The Mess That Made Them

The Mess That Made Them

How History's Greatest Artists Failed, Floundered, and Made Something Brilliant Anyway

Ryan T. Pozzi

BLOOMSBURY ACADEMIC
NEW YORK • LONDON • OXFORD • NEW DELHI • SYDNEY

BLOOMSBURY ACADEMIC
Bloomsbury Publishing Inc, 1359 Broadway, New York, NY 10018, USA
Bloomsbury Publishing Plc, 50 Bedford Square, London, WC1B 3DP, UK
Bloomsbury Publishing Ireland, 29 Earlsfort Terrace, Dublin 2, D02 AY28, Ireland

First published in the United States of America 2026

Cover design: Jen Huppert
Cover image © iStock.com/master1305

A catalog record for this book is available from the Library of Congress.

ISBN: HB: 979-8-216-38247-8
ePDF: 979-8-216-38249-2
eBook: 979-8-216-38248-5

Typeset by Integra Software Services Pvt. Ltd.
Printed and bound in the United States of America

For product safety related questions contact productsafety@bloomsbury.com.

To find out more about our authors and books visit www.bloomsbury.com and sign up for our newsletters.

Contents

Author's Note

Before You Begin

Thank you for being here. Let's handle some brief but important housekeeping to help everyone stay safe and happy throughout our tale. If you habitually roll your eyes at this sort of thing, don't waste your energy on hate mail. Just skip ahead to the Prelude and we'll all get on with our lives. For those to whom this does matter, I love this book, but you matter more. If you need to stop reading at any point, please do.

Love & Rockets. RTP

Human Authored™, Reg #: 7155982, https://authorsguild.org/human

Content Warning

This book contains sensitive material, including references to violence; suicidal ideation and death by suicide; mass killing in wartime; and mental illness, including hallucinations. Some readers may find this content distressing. If you need support, call or text 988 to reach the 988 Suicide & Crisis Lifeline in the United States and Canada or call 111 to reach the NHS 111 Helpline in the United Kingdom.

Prelude

I've spent most of my life obsessed with the mess behind greatness: artists who struggled, failed spectacularly, and sometimes wrecked themselves completely in the process of creating something extraordinary. I keep circling back to one question. Why do they keep going when everything tells them to stop? And, if I'm honest, why do I need to believe in that so badly?

Books were my first great escape. Sleep felt like punishment, and bedtime was my nightly opponent. My mother, ever the strategist, offered a deal: lights out at nine unless I had a chapter book. If I was reading, the bendy snake light stayed on until ten. I didn't love books yet, but she saw the opening in my battle against sleep and took it. It worked.

I worried constantly about running out of books. Reading became an obsessive logistical operation, managed with the precision other kids applied to baseball cards or action figures. Deep down, I wanted to write my own stories, but authors felt impossibly distant, like mythic beings who turned words into worlds. I was a geeky disabled kid with oversized glasses and a limp. Becoming one of them seemed about as likely as getting picked first on the playground. It took nearly forty years for me to give myself permission to try.

Not long after my discovery of books, my mom married a man who loved classical music. Not casually. Obsessively. A euphonium player devoted to Sousa marches. At first, I didn't get it. To me, classical music was the nap-time soundtrack Mrs. Feathergill used to knock out a classroom of second-graders. I preferred stomping, shouting, and any activity that did not involve finesse.

But my stepdad was persistent. Then one day, as *Semper Fidelis* bounced along in the background, he said, "Did you know Sousa never wanted to be a Marine? He dreamed of playing violin under the big top. His father enlisted him just to keep him from running away to join the circus." Then he went back to tapping along with the music, as if he hadn't just cracked open a hidden door in my brain I didn't even know was there.

Those marches, once just background noise, suddenly filled with tumbling clowns, roaring lions, and daring trapeze artists. Knowing something real about Sousa made the music electric. Without realizing it, I'd discovered the thread that would pull me through the rest of my life: art isn't just about what it is. It's about who made it, and why.

In 2012, half a dozen years into my own creative life and career, I found myself in the nation's capital, inches from one of van Gogh's final self-portraits, completely overwhelmed. Without thinking, I did what no responsible adult should ever do. I leaned in and sniffed the painting. In my defense, the gallery was closing, and I might never get this close to Vincent again. I wanted to take in something deeper than colors and brushstrokes. Security had a different view. What I called art appreciation, they called "dangerous" and "probably illegal." If I'd sneezed, I'd be known not as a writer, but as the man who nose-punched a van Gogh. They promptly showed me the door. Gently, yes, but with the unmistakable energy of people who've practiced this exact maneuver before.

I knew better than to sniff the painting. I just couldn't help myself. It was foolish, even reckless, but it didn't feel optional. It was my way of reaching toward someone who knew how it felt to pour yourself into the work and be ignored, dismissed, or erased. His painting, raw and unguarded, made me feel seen. I floated more than walked away from that portrait, although technically, I guess I was *being walked*.

Back then, my visual art knowledge was mostly a collection of anecdotes and personal favorites. Composers and authors were more my speed. When I married Elizabeth, a visual artist herself, everything shifted. She saw more depth than I did. To her, visual artists were people trying to shape meaning from a world that rarely makes sense.

She didn't discourage my obsessions. One day, she asked, "Did I ever tell you Picasso was accused of stealing the Mona Lisa?" A week later, I resurfaced from a research spiral with a corkboard full of thumbtacks and red string. Obviously, we were going to solve this caper.

When I finally decided to write about the strange lives of creative people, I didn't want to make them look tidy or impressive. I wanted to understand what it costs to keep creating, especially when nothing guarantees that anyone will care. I started with the artists who fascinated me as a kid. Somewhere along the way, I realized I wasn't just collecting biographies. I was tracing something else entirely. This had to be a book about what it means to keep going when it's hard, thankless, and especially when no one's watching.

We'll meet composers, painters, and writers whose lives were anything but orderly. Many were overlooked, silenced, broken, or dismissed and yet they kept going. A few believed in themselves. Others never did. For some, belief had nothing to do with it, but all of them made something that outlasted their moment.

This book isn't about genius. In fact, in it, I argue that genius, as we tend to understand it, is a myth. It would be truer to say that it's about grit. It's about what it takes to keep reaching for meaning when all the evidence suggests it isn't worth it. These stories are here to get honest about what art actually demands. Brilliance is overrated. Perfection is a lie. What lasts often starts in silence.

If you've ever doubted your voice or wondered whether the work is worth it, just as I have many times, this book was written with you in mind. We begin, as we must, with someone who broke every conceivable rule and built something no one expected would last. It almost didn't.

Refusal as a Beginning

When the first step forward is to say no and the whole shape of a life bends around that choice.

CARAVAGGIO | MODEST MUSSORGSKY | OSCAR WILDE | FRÉDÉRIC CHOPIN

Caravaggio

Let's start in Malta, where Caravaggio held a weapon instead of a brush. He had just been knighted by the Order of Saint John, a rare honor for a painter. He celebrated by insulting another knight, picking a fight, and nearly beating the man to death with a length of iron pipe. That's no metaphor. He left the knight bleeding on the ground and disappeared. The Order was outraged. Assaulting a fellow knight was an unthinkable offense. He was arrested, imprisoned, and stripped of his title, but Caravaggio had no intention of staying put. He literally broke through the walls of his locked cell, escaped the fortress, and vanished into the night.

Even for Caravaggio, this was bold. A man wanted for murder in Rome was now exiled from Malta with a second major crime to his name, and a rapidly shrinking list of places willing to hide him. He drifted through Sicily and Naples, painting when he could. Here's a masterpiece. Maybe let me live here? He was desperate to get back to Rome, but he was also still Caravaggio. He couldn't stop provoking people.

Just a year earlier, he'd killed a man named Ranuccio Tomassoni. Officially, it was over a disputed tennis match, but scholars think it was something closer to a duel. The court records describe a violent exchange in a public square. Tomassoni died of a stab wound to the groin, likely intended to injure, not kill. Caravaggio fled the city before the death sentence could be carried out. From that point on, he was a moving target.

This is where we find him as the chapter begins: dangerous, brilliant, exiled, and running out of favors. He sent paintings ahead as offerings and bribes, hoping to reach those with the power to erase his troubles. It didn't work. The charges stood and Caravaggio, the brilliant, erratic, violent painter who helped invent the Baroque, never made it home. He died somewhere along the coast at thirty-eight. We're still not sure exactly where or how, which, given the rest of his life, feels about right.

Caravaggio lived like someone always ready to fight. Yet, for all his volatility, Caravaggio's work is full of stillness. Still bodies, still light, moments of silence stretched to their limit. This is the stillness right before something breaks. You can feel it in his David, where the boy holds Goliath's head, Caravaggio's own face, and the look is closer to pity than triumph.

Art in Caravaggio's day was supposed to idealize. It could be dramatic, but not dirty. Sacred, but not scary. The figures in religious paintings were meant to look holy, refined, removed from anything that might feel too close to real life. Caravaggio ignored all of that. He painted saints with calloused feet and creased brows. Mary looked exhausted. Peter looked terrified. Matthew, in one of his most famous commissions, doesn't even recognize that he's being called by Christ. He points to his own chest as if to say, "Who, me? Surely not."

His scenes unfold in heavy shadow, with sharp directional light slicing across the canvas like a stage spotlight that got caught mid-movement. You can almost feel the sweat. These paintings were meant to stare you down. Caravaggio used realism as a weapon to make the viewer uneasy, never seeking to comfort.

You can see it in *The Incredulity of Saint Thomas* (Plate 1). Thomas doesn't just observe Christ's wound; he touches it. Rather than the moment of realization or revelation, Caravaggio shows the moment of physical proof. Jesus, calm and still, parts his robe and guides Thomas' hand inside the open wound beneath his ribs. The gesture is surgical. Thomas peers in like a man inspecting a broken hinge. His brow is furrowed, his fingers are buried knuckle-deep in flesh. You can almost hear the quiet wetness of the scene.

No one expected this in Rome in 1601. This wasn't how sacred moments were supposed to look. Caravaggio could've pulled the viewer back a few feet, obscured the contact, and let the drama rise gently. Instead, he zoomed all the way in. He gave us skin, and pressure, and the instant before belief takes hold. The closeness was what made the painting dangerous. There's no room to romanticize Christ here. No golden glow. No shining features. Just the exhausted face of a man who was killed and got back up and, in front of him, a doubter who has to feel his way back to faith.

People hated it. Church officials worried the figures looked too common, too dirty, too alive. Religious patrons refused finished commissions. Other artists accused him of not knowing how to draw. His paintings were so grounded in the model that they claimed he couldn't compose from imagination. For all his innovation, Caravaggio made the elite deeply uncomfortable. He didn't care. This was art for people who knew what grief felt like in their bodies. A kind of grief that leaves you bent at the waist, that takes weeks to crawl out of. His paintings never ask you to admire their subjects. They ask you to recognize them and to see yourself in them. If you can't, they dare you to look closer.

Today, we praise this as revolutionary, but at the time, it was a kind of defiance that put him at constant risk because Caravaggio wasn't just painting religious subjects. He was making sacred things look human, taking the Church's tightly guarded symbols and pulling them down into the streets. Nothing is more dangerous, then or now, than turning something that the powerful control into something the public might relate to.

It wasn't just the threat of his style that worried his contemporaries. Caravaggio was a literal threat. He was arrested for carrying a sword without a permit. Arrested again for carrying it anyway. He once started a fistfight with a waiter over a plate of artichokes. Some were cooked in butter, others in oil, and that was apparently enough to ruin his entire day. He insulted the wrong man in the street and got slashed across the face, hard enough to mark him for life. Frankly, he attracted trouble, as if his whole world were tilted toward confrontation.

Even his allies found him exhausting. One of his Roman patrons, the art dealer and connoisseur Giovanni Baglione, admired his talent but eventually turned on him and then painted a near-direct copy of one of Caravaggio's compositions out of spite. The two men launched a pamphlet war, trading insults in print, accusing each other of blasphemy, fraud, and worse. Baglione even published a thinly veiled biography that framed Caravaggio as spiritually and morally corrupt. Other patrons tried to keep him on a leash with generous commissions, but it rarely worked. He missed deadlines and fought with clients, even refusing on occasion to deliver paintings that had already been paid for. In other words, he was a professional risk. Painters who worked in the era's studio system could fulfill bulk commissions on time, churn out altar scenes, handle retouching, and maintain relationships. Caravaggio was a freelancer with a violent streak. Supporting him meant signing up for scandal. When the painting arrived, it might be a masterpiece, or it might never come at all.

One patron described him as having a "melancholy and fantastic humor," which was seventeenth-century Italian for "a nightmare to work with." He never lasted long in one place, and he stirred conflict everywhere he went. Most artists at the time were part of that studio system, protected, trained, and employed through networks of commissions and apprenticeships. Caravaggio rejected all of it. He trained briefly, then struck out alone, barely scraped by, and clawed his way to fame by painting better than anyone else, and refusing to be ignored, no matter the cost.

Caravaggio skipped the sketches and the prep work. He pulled models from the street and set them right into sacred scenes. Some were prostitutes, others beggars, but all of them were real. The Church tried to civilize him by offering prestige, patronage, and proximity to power. Caravaggio responded by painting their saints with the faces of their own outcasts.

There's a tendency to frame all this as mythic now, to cast him as a dark romantic archetype: the tormented genius, the rebel artist, the haunted man who turned pain into brilliance. The reality was more dangerous. People got hurt. He fled legal charges, and there's evidence he committed murder at least once before Tomassoni. None of that disappears just because the paintings are good.

And yet the paintings are better than just good. They cut through centuries of tradition and land on something raw, something still alive. Reckless, violent, even monstrous, he had no interest in playing nice or in making art that soothed. Sometimes, when the whole world pushes you to behave, there's a strange kind of power in refusing to be manageable. It's tempting to say Caravaggio was all instinct and impulse, but that's not true either. His life may have spiraled, but the work never did. His compositions are deliberate, studied, and exacting. Every gesture, every shadow, every shaft of light is precisely where it needs to be. The drama was real, but none of it was careless.

I think that makes it harder to dismiss him. He's not just another talented mess spiraling into legend, because the work refuses that reading. The paintings hold up not only on technical grounds but on emotional ones. Where most of his contemporaries painted devotional altarpieces meant to sit on the wall like shrines, he staged scenes that feel as if they are mid-action. You can sense the camera angles and hear the breath in the room. Even his stillness feels deliberate, like it's waiting for a cue that never comes. There's control in that kind of restraint, a clarity that comes only from someone who knows exactly what effect they're after. For all his violence, Caravaggio's art was deliberate. Every stroke found its mark.

I feel it in *The Entombment of Christ.* Caravaggio gives us six figures: Mary, Mary Magdalene, Nicodemus, John, a grieving mother, and the dead weight of Christ himself. They look wrecked, not holy. This is a scene of raw, human grief caught in the instant before collapse. Christ's body hangs like a slab of meat, heavy and pale, nearly sliding off the stone beneath him. His arm dangles and his mouth is slack. The hands that carry him struggle under the heaviness of both the body and the moment. The composition is carefully staged, and the figures form a downward diagonal, drawing the eye toward Christ's feet and the stone beneath him. At the center is the outstretched hand of Nicodemus, fingers spread in a gesture of helpless explanation. It's as if he's offering the scene to us directly: Look. This happened.

The light cuts in hard, exposing every wrinkle, every fold of cloth, and every trace of exhaustion. There's nothing accidental about any of it. This was emotional choreography, and it only works because Caravaggio knew exactly where to put the pain. That makes the whole picture more complicated because if he had no control, then he's just a casualty of his own chaos, but he did have control, he just didn't apply it to the rest of his life. He could dial in precision, order, and meaning at will. Still, he chose, over and over, to live like the fallout would never catch him.

That's a harder story. We like clean arcs, the flawed genius redeemed, the troubled soul saved by beauty, but Caravaggio doesn't give us that. He gives us someone who could get it right and doesn't, someone who creates transcendent things but burns through every chance to keep making them. Maybe that's part of what makes the paintings hit me so hard. What we're seeing isn't just what he made, it's what it cost him to make it. It's heartbreaking to look at someone's greatest work and know he didn't get to come with it. The art made it. He didn't.

By the end, even Caravaggio seemed to know he was running out of time. He tried to get back to Rome and secure a pardon, tried to go home. He sent a final painting ahead of him, *David with the Head of Goliath*, with his own face painted onto the severed head. It was more than a gesture, more than an admission or a plea. It was, in its way, a kind of self-sentencing.

He died before the pardon arrived, alone and on the road to Rome at just thirty-eight. The circumstances remain unclear. Some say fever, others suggest murder or poisoning. His body was buried in an unmarked grave near Porto Ercole, the Church never issued an official pardon, and his name wasn't restored. For a long time, neither was his place in history. His paintings were just too raw, his life too unsavory. For decades, his name nearly vanished from major collections and surveys of art history. Other painters borrowed from him freely: his lighting, his realism, his intensity, but without the blood under the fingernails. Caravaggio's name became shorthand for scandal, and his brilliance was buried with him.

The next generation of painters made the saints beautiful again. They erased the sweat, the wrinkles, the street-level grit and Caravaggio's shadows went out of style. His subjects became too raw, too strange, too close to the bone. He was seen as a problem, on canvas as well as off but his fingerprints show up everywhere. You can trace him in Rembrandt, in Velázquez, in Gentileschi. It shows in lighting, but also in the refusal to look away or in the decision to get too close. His influence is there every time an artist leaves pain visible on screen or canvas. You can feel it in filmmakers like Scorsese and self-described Caravaggio devotee Derek Jarman, in photographers like Nan Goldin, in painters who refuse to separate suffering from beauty. It reaches into the chiaroscuro of graphic novels, crime cinema, and underground theater. Any time someone takes something sacred and drags it through the dirt without letting it go, Caravaggio is in the room.

There's no redemption arc, no noble final act, only the body of a man lost somewhere on the road back and a body of work that took centuries to be fully understood. That's the part people try to clean up. The art world keeps trying to make Caravaggio look respectable, to separate the man from the scandal, but they're inseparable. He didn't make masterpieces in spite of his volatility. He made them through it.

Don't mistake me. I'm not saying the ends justify the means. We romanticize self-destruction far too easily, especially in artists. But it's worth asking: what do you do with someone who fought every system he touched, hurt people along the way, and still made something that shook the world? There's no easy answer, but maybe the point isn't to forgive him or to judge him. Maybe it's just to look at what he made and admit what it cost him and everyone around him. Then we can ask what we're actually willing to celebrate—and why.

I didn't see a Caravaggio in person until I was well into adulthood. The first time I remember really looking at one was in a battered art history textbook, a reproduction of *The Taking of Christ*. It's a scene I knew: Judas betrays Jesus with a kiss, but I wasn't ready for how close the painting was. There's no distance or serenity. Just faces twisted in panic and grief and the sudden knowledge that something irreversible has happened. One soldier grips Christ's arm with fingers dug into the muscle, forcing him forward. It feels too real. It made me uncomfortable not because it was violent, but because it felt like I was there, like I'd accidentally walked into the scene mid-betrayal. I didn't know how to look at something that direct. I was used to beauty that kept its distance. This one grabbed me, pulled me in close, and didn't let go.

At the time, I didn't have words for why that mattered. I just knew it was different, and that I couldn't stop thinking about it. Years later, when I finally started writing about art, I came back to that painting. Still uncomfortable and too close, but now I understood the power in that closeness. Caravaggio wanted us to feel implicated.

His life, first and foremost, is a warning for people like us. You don't have to destroy yourself to make something honest but it's also a reminder that obedience isn't the only way to make an impact. He ignored the rules, resisted flattery, and never worked to make himself acceptable.

Still, he changed everything.

We learn to behave, cooperate, and compromise. These habits are rewarded if we want to be taken seriously or heard but sometimes, the thing that matters most, the thing that feels truest in your hands, won't survive being made acceptable.

That doesn't mean you have to burn it all down. It means you get very clear on what's worth fighting for, and what's just there to keep you small. If you fight everything, you lose the thread but if you don't fight at all, you lose yourself. Caravaggio fought everyone and everything, sometimes even his own best interests. No one managed to contain him. There is a pull in that refusal, messy and brutal as it was, that still draws us closer.

You don't have to be like him, and you shouldn't. He burned bridges and caused real harm, and no one should admire that. Still, if there's something that won't fit into polite conversation or curated timelines or quarterly goals, you already know what the pressure to behave feels like. We're told to be manageable in art and even more in life. The world rewards us when we play along. Each time we smooth over what we mean to say, with every adjustment for acceptability, we risk losing something we might never recover.

Caravaggio rejected every bit of that risk. His way was messy and unapologetic. He kept his work large, never letting the rules shrink him. Caravaggio wouldn't be discussed today if the saints had clean feet in his paintings. That's the part worth stealing – the nerve to leave the work raw where it mattered most.

Modest Mussorgsky

Let's start with the edits.

Modest Mussorgsky was dead when the real damage began. He'd written the greatest work of his life, *Boris Godunov*, a jagged, unruly opera with unorthodox melodies and speech-like rhythms that sounded like no one else. It was too Russian, too unrefined, too much. Critics said it lacked polish, and composers said it lacked discipline. So his peers rewrote it.

Rimsky-Korsakov, a friend and fellow composer, took it upon himself to "correct" the opera. He cleaned up the harmonies, bought the unruly genius into line with what music was supposed to sound like. For over a century, that was the version the world heard. The result wasn't Mussorgsky's voice at all, just a tidied-up approximation.

It didn't stop there. His songs were rearranged and his scores reorchestrated. Ravel turned *Pictures at an Exhibition* into a shimmering orchestral showpiece. It was a beautiful theft. The original, written for solo piano, was something else entirely. It was spiky, personal, and strange. It rattled with motion and mourned with restraint, but the cleaned-up version made it feel more sophisticated. More European. More right. This is the version that survived.

If you can get past the betrayal, it's easy to see why that was. Mussorgsky's music ignored the rules of harmony and trampled over proper technique. It let people stumble, strain, and break mid-thought, trusting feeling over form even when the result turned messy. His work sounded wrong to the ears of his time. Even his friends said so. But he wasn't wrong, he was just early. He was writing for a Russia that didn't exist, for a world that could absorb dissonance and find truth in musical phrases that refused to resolve. The world wasn't there yet. It wasn't ready for him, so it reshaped him into something it could tolerate.

That's where we begin, with the idea that someone else always thinks they know better. When something feels wild, strange, or unfinished, the instinct is to polish it, to smooth out the rough edges until it looks like everything else. It works, but it's also how we trade away what made it original.

Mussorgsky's music didn't sound the way it was supposed to, it lurched and surged, wandered off rhythm, and let characters interrupt themselves. His harmonies clashed and buckled under pressure. Where traditional composers built cathedrals, Mussorgsky shook the ground beneath them, less architecture than aftershock.

There's a moment in *Boris Godunov*, his epic opera, where the grandeur of royalty gives way to the desperation of madness. The tsar, plagued by guilt, descends into a kind of broken prayer. Mussorgsky doesn't give him the traditional soaring aria. He lets his mind unravel in front of us. The rhythms are irregular, the melody twists, and the whole thing feels like listening to someone trying, and slowly failing, to hold himself together.

Then there's *Pictures at an Exhibition*. Originally written for solo piano, it's a walk through grief, a tribute to his dead friend Viktor Hartmann, whose sketches inspired each piece. The music ignores formal structure, staggering from painting to painting, moving from heavy-footed processions to manic flights. The "Promenade" theme keeps returning, as if Mussorgsky himself were pacing the gallery, overwhelmed. Where Ravel's orchestration made it a jaunty crowd-pleaser, Mussorgsky's version feels like mourning in motion.

Even his songs are strange. His *Songs and Dances of Death* are lullabies for the end of the line. One is sung from the perspective of Death himself, gently rocking a sick child. The piano sways like a cradle. Another shows Death as a seductive dancer, luring a woman into stillness. In the final song, Death walks a battlefield among the fallen, calm and inevitable, collecting the bodies one by one. Mussorgsky wrote music that spoke in slurred syllables and ragged breaths, letting grief sound tired and even kings fall apart. He made space for sounds that refused refinement, because the feelings behind them weren't refined either. It wasn't perfect or clean, but it was true.

People heard this and assumed he didn't know what he was doing. They called him careless, untrained, a noble amateur. Even those who admired him treated him as raw material, a man with instincts but no discipline. They missed the point. He wasn't chasing correctness. What he wanted was humanity. Mussorgsky knew the rules and chose to break them, not out of ignorance but because they excluded the very people he thought they should have welcomed.

Modest came from privilege, but he never played the part well. He was born into minor Russian nobility and trained at military school. His family expected him to climb the officer ranks, not chase music. He did both for a while. Served in a prestigious regiment by day, wrote music by night, and drank too much through it all. By his twenties, he was already spiraling. He quit the military, lost his income, and started a slow drift through government jobs, couch-surfing arrangements, and stretches of real poverty.

He looked like a man unraveling, with stained clothes and unkempt hair. One critic called him "half-crazed," and by the end of his life that image stuck: Mussorgsky as the disheveled failure, the brilliant wreck. But that version is too easy. He may have been falling apart, but he was also trying, again and again, to build something new.

Mussorgsky wanted his music to sound like Russia, not the imperial Russia of courts and salons, but the Russia of peasants, street songs, spoken rhythms, and kitchen tables. He once said he wanted to "recreate human speech in music," and that became his obsession. Reality was his goal, not beauty. He listened for speech patterns and village chants, studied the way people talked when they were grieving, praying, arguing, or drinking. What he cared about was the rhythm beneath it all, the way a singer's voice could waver like someone struggling to hold themselves steady. It made him hard to categorize. He wasn't interested in beauty for its own sake, and he had no use for respectability. What he kept reaching for was something slippery and strange, something that sounded more like real life.

He had too much training to be considered a folk composer, but too much chaos to be treated like a formal one. He was betweenness in human form. Too refined to be dismissed but too unruly to be embraced, he was treated as a failure. The problem wasn't the work itself. The problem was that the systems and the colleagues around him had no idea how to understand what he made.

His letters reveal a man full of contradictions, fiery one moment and heavy with shame the next. He worried about money and about not belonging in the very world he was trying to change, yet he never let go of the belief that it was the music that needed to change, not him. He could be sharp, funny, and fiercely loyal, sometimes giving his last ruble to a friend. At the same time, the drinking worsened, the depression deepened, and loss surrounded him. He tried to recover, but relapse followed him like a shadow.

In the final days, he bounced between unstable living situations, his health in steady decline. He was hospitalized again, weak and drinking even then. There's a portrait of him from those last moments, painted by Ilya Repin just days before his death (Plate 2). Mussorgsky is propped up in a hospital bed, wild-haired, with eyes that still spark. His beard is scraggly and his clothes hang loose, yet he faces forward with a stubborn, electric gaze. The portrait doesn't read as tragedy. It reads as a man still defiant, even at the end.

That's what people missed. The tragedy was the fact that no one knew what to do with a man who refused to be fixed. The world wavered between ridicule and pity. Some critics mocked him, others dismissed him with condescension, and even admirers tended to treat him like a project, raw talent that needed shaping, a so-called primitive who might someday grow into a proper composer.

It was never really about the ideas. It was about the form. His instincts were praised only after they were rewritten. The songs were worth saving, people said, if someone else corrected the harmony. The opera *Boris Godunov* was called powerful, but only once Rimsky-Korsakov "restored" it. Mussorgsky kept being labeled ahead of his time, though never in a way that let him remain himself. The compliment always implied that he might have arrived if he had behaved, cleaned up, or waited his turn. He didn't wait. He wrote the way he wanted, and the world called it failure instead of courage. The real cost was erasure. His work kept being reshaped until it no longer felt like his. Rough edges were polished away, honesty buried under performance, and the strangeness that made it Mussorgsky was the first thing to go.

It's easy to celebrate innovation in hindsight. In its own time, though, it usually looks like disobedience. It bends the arc, sounds wrong, and unsettles the people who guard the canon. When the discomfort becomes too much for them, their usual response is to smooth it out, to call it "maturity" or "editing" or "preservation," and to make it safer for them than it really was. That's what Rimsky-Korsakov did, not out of cruelty, but out of condescension. He couldn't accept that music so unruly, so emotional, so uneven, might still be right. So he straightened it, polished it, and turned it classical. He thought he was rescuing it, but what he really did was smother it until Mussorgsky's voice was barely audible.

The polished versions won. For more than a century, the Mussorgsky most people heard was Mussorgsky corrected. Rimsky-Korsakov's edits became the standard, and Ravel's *Pictures at an Exhibition* became the expectation. Entire generations learned the altered versions first, if they heard the originals at all. What endured was less Mussorgsky himself than the supposed brilliance of those who claimed to have "rescued" him.

Rimsky-Korsakov was praised for his taste, his technique, and his ability to turn rough genius into refined art. Ravel's orchestration became a concert hall staple: lush, colorful, easy to love. Both men were celebrated as bridges between raw instinct and respectable form. But look closer. That isn't a bridge. It's a gate. Teaching Mussorgsky through their edits doesn't introduce him. It introduces the people who refused to trust his voice on its own.

This is how it happens, over and over. An artist does something bold. The world resists. We call in the experts and the work gets fixed. Then the fixers get celebrated for making it more palatable. This isn't a story about music. It's a story about power. Legacy is about what you make, but it's also about what people allow to survive. What survives isn't always the most important or most creative part. It's whatever slips neatly into the existing frame, the pieces that sound familiar, the versions that don't unsettle too many people. History tends to reward the stories it already knows how to tell: tidy arcs, clean resolutions, names that behave. Mussorgsky's work refused to behave, so instead of shifting the frame, they reshaped the work. Erasure rarely needs outright censorship. Most of the time, convenience does the work. You don't have to ban something to make it vanish. You just have to replace it with something easier to explain. Mussorgsky's work was raw, unapologetically Russian, and difficult to explain. To be fair, not everyone who touched his scores was plotting to erase him. Friends like Rimsky-Korsakov honestly believed they were rescuing a brilliant but unruly composer from himself, "correcting" what they saw as technical weaknesses so the music could survive on major stages. We know this not from legend, but from the scores and piano pieces he left behind, from the original *Boris Godunov* and the unsmoothed *Pictures at an Exhibition*, with their jagged harmonies and speech-like vocal lines. The very things his contemporaries heard as crude are what later composers and critics recognized as visionary. He refused to flatter the imperial aesthetic or compose for a European ear. He refused to behave. So they revised him, sanitized him, lifted his name, but muffled his voice.

Over the last century, the balance has shifted. Musicologists now describe Mussorgsky as one of the foremost masters of musical realism, pointing to vocal lines that follow everyday speech and harmonies that fracture with the drama instead of gliding over it. Program notes talk about the unedited *Pictures at an Exhibition* as beautiful and unmistakably original in its roughness, not a failed draft that needed to be cleaned up. Major opera companies and orchestras that once relied on revised, "corrected" editions of *Boris Godunov* now often return to Mussorgsky's own versions, drawn to the rugged individuality of his orchestration and harmony.

Shostakovich reorchestrated *Boris Godunov* and folded Mussorgsky's harsh, wintry realism into his own symphonies. Debussy admired the way Mussorgsky broke from European decorum, especially in the speech-like pull of his vocal writing. Ravel and Stravinsky joined in reworking *Khovanshchina* for Diaghilev, a collaboration that doubled as a kind of tribute to the raw material they clearly considered worth saving.

Even with that slow correction, there is still a reflex to treat his originals as experiments rather than as a standard. Critics still speculate about what he might have become if he'd survived longer, worked harder, or tamed his drinking. That way of thinking erases what was already there: the wild brilliance, the emotional honesty, the musical logic that refused to fit inside small rules. Mussorgsky wasn't unfinished. He was already doing the work. It was the frame around him that refused to change.

This isn't just Mussorgsky's story. You've felt it. The moment someone offers to help, but only if you'll tone it down first. The praise with conditions. The doors that open, then shut the second you step through as your authentic self instead of as the version of you that the world prefers. That's what happened to him. He was loved, but only in edited form. Respected, but only through someone else's filter. He was remembered, but not for what he actually made. We still do this. We reward originality when it's polished. We admire strangeness as long as it sells. We cheer for boldness until it stops entertaining us.

That's what makes this so hard to spot in the moment. It feels like support, like guidance, like someone doing you a favor. Sometimes they're right. Other times, what gets edited out are the parts they don't understand, the parts that don't test well, the ones that won't move units fast enough. And it's not just artists who face this. It's anyone who lives a little out of step, who doesn't clean up well, who gets called a mess when really, they're just refusing to stick to the script. That's the risk of polish. Not the polish itself, but what happens when polish becomes the only measure of worth. Every wild thing has to be sanded, shaped, and made safe before anyone will call it great.

And yet, Mussorgsky's story isn't a model to follow. He was brilliant and unstable, loyal at times but quick to sabotage himself. He pushed people away, wasted chances, and left behind enough chaos that rewriting him seemed easier than understanding him. What mattered most was what got erased. The world wasn't only reacting to the drinking or the disorder. It was reacting to his refusal to sound the way he was supposed to, to write what he was told, to become the composer he might have been if he had changed, waited, or allowed himself to be shaped. He didn't and the cost fell on the music. The music itself never failed. The failure was in the world's refusal to see it for what it was.

So here's the truth that's hardest to face: The thing they tried to fix might have been the thing that made it great. We don't like it because it means we have to sit with our discomfort. Of course, some notes make the work more itself. The best edits sharpen what is already alive instead of sanding it down. What I am talking about here is something different. We have to question whether the versions of ourselves we present to the world are actually ours, or just more acceptable edits. Maybe you've been there. Someone praises your potential, then offers notes on how to be more digestible. They tell you to tone it down, to make it cleaner, to make it make sense. There's help if you're willing to be corrected, and maybe you take it. You take the notes, smooth it out, shrink it down. You call it compromise, convince yourself it's growth, or pretend it's strategy. But something goes quiet and something gets smaller. Maybe it's still there, waiting, some raw part of you that wasn't broken at all, only inconvenient.

That's the part of you this chapter is for. Not because Mussorgsky was always right, and not because refinement is always the enemy. It's because you deserve to know the difference between help and containment, and you deserve the choice of what gets shaped and what stays yours.

Sometimes the mess is the masterpiece. Don't rush to clean up what was never broken. Hold on to the thing that resists order. Keep the idea that doesn't sound finished yet, the story that won't quiet down. Let it stay jagged. Let it stay strange. Claim the space no one meant to give it because the piece they try to fix might be the one piece that changes everything. If they fix it without your blessing: Make another. Make it louder and stranger. Let it exist without apology because if the world asks you to be clearer, that might just be a clever euphemism for being smaller. When it asks you to be more refined, it often means to be less like yourself. When the world says it doesn't sound quite right, ask who they expected it to sound like if not you.

Don't misunderstand me. This isn't an argument for chaos, and it isn't a plea to treat every rough edge as sacred. Mussorgsky's example matters because the thing they kept correcting was the thing that made the music his. Rimsky-Korsakov could make it smoother, but he could never make it more Mussorgsky.

Oscar Wilde

He made himself impossible to miss with velvet jackets instead of black wool and lavender gloves instead of stiff collars. A voice that refused to settle for silence or dullness. He carried himself like a provocation, as if every gesture were a dare.

Wilde weaponized charm, turning wit into both shield and sword. Critics found themselves undone not by arguments but by his speed, and the way he could twist a phrase until it sparkled. Performance for him was more than style, it was a philosophy. When people pressed him on whether he meant the outrageous things he said, he answered with a grin and a line: "The first duty in life is to assume a pose. What the second duty is, no one has yet found out." He orchestrated his fame in a way that was uncommon for his time. His wit landed him on stages, in newspapers, and in royal company. He understood that the louder they laughed, the more he could get away with saying, so he made people laugh, and then he snuck in the truth.

Even Wilde's greatest success, *The Importance of Being Earnest*, is built on that same tension between surface and substance. It's a farce about mistaken identities, hidden names, and invented lives, but underneath the satire is something quieter and more biting: the suggestion that people might live fuller, freer lives if they weren't required to pretend. Wilde once said that "man is least himself when he talks in his own person. Give him a mask, and he will tell you the truth." It's what he did without the mask that told the real story. He insisted on being seen. Wilde didn't stumble into visibility. He cultivated it by accident. Attention was the point, not the by-product. What unsettled people most was that he refused to hide.

He performed in public but he also performed on the page. Every sentence he published was stylized, sharpened, and dangerously precise. His plays were comedies of manners built like traps. Characters danced through high society, trading clever barbs and pretending not to care, until someone slipped and said something real. The point was always for the truth to arrive dressed as a joke.

Even when Wilde wrote about beauty, he wasn't embellishing, he was dismantling. *The Picture of Dorian Gray* is remembered as a gothic morality tale, but under the surface it's much harder to pin down. It reads as a defense of pleasure, a veiled confession, and a mirror held up to anyone who has ever wanted to live one way and appear another. Critics called it decadent, amoral, even poisonous. One review dismissed it as "a tale spawned from the leprous literature of the French decadents." Wilde, unbothered, answered that the book was never meant to be moral at all. "Books," he said, "are well written, or badly written. That is all."

They knew there was more to it, and so did he. The novel carried a charge that couldn't be disguised. Its was in the way it asked readers to look at beauty, temptation, and desire between men as something real, complicated, and fully human instead of a passing sin. Wilde hadn't hidden it enough for the world he lived in, or perhaps he hadn't wanted to. Either way, the effect was the same: he stopped being a spectacle and became a problem.

Wilde wrote Dorian Gray as a revelation, first to himself and then to anyone willing to read between the lines. The novel thrums with duality: beauty turning to rot, youth shadowed by consequence, a polished surface stretched over hidden truth. Dorian's portrait ages while he stays young, and the device doubles as confession. Wilde was showing what it meant to wear one face for the world while another, more dangerous self, stared back from the canvas. The story was as much about Wilde as it was about Dorian. He once said, "Basil Hallward is what I think I am; Lord Henry what the world thinks me; Dorian what I would like to be—in other ages, perhaps." He left breadcrumbs in the margins and confidences inside the fiction. It wasn't subtle, which may be why it wasn't safe, either.

Wilde used epigrams as armor, keeping people guessing about where he really stood. "I can resist everything except temptation." "The only way to get rid of a temptation is to yield to it." "To love oneself is the beginning of a lifelong romance." Each one was delivered with charm and precision, but each one pointing somewhere deeper.

His work walked the line between spectacle and sedition. The laughter bought him time while the applause bought him access. The words were doing something more dangerous: they were making people look at what they'd been trained to avoid, the love and longing between men that Victorian respectability pretended didn't exist. His art was as brave as it was beautiful, and he paid for every line of it.

He should have left when danger came calling. He could have fled to France or Italy and lived out his days in relative safety, surrounded by friends and art and admiration. But Oscar Wilde didn't run. By then his relationship with Lord Alfred Douglas wasn't a whisper anymore. Everyone knew. Douglas's father, the Marquess of Queensberry, had already threatened Wilde publicly, left calling cards accusing him of "posing as a sodomite," and tried to crash the opening night of *The Importance of Being Earnest* with a bouquet of rotting vegetables.

Wilde sued him for libel. He walked into court wearing carnations and wit, believing fatally that the truth would protect him. It was a mistake. The trial turned into a theater of humiliation. Wilde was cross-examined on the "immorality" of his writing. Private letters were read aloud. Lovers were named. The same wit that once dazzled now made him look evasive and even cruel. Juries are not known for rewarding flamboyance under pressure. His case collapsed.

Queensberry was acquitted. Wilde was arrested. Visibility no longer offered power; now it offered proof. He was convicted of "gross indecency" and sentenced to two years of hard labor.

Prison left Wilde in pieces. The hard labor wrecked his body, and the silence wrecked everything else. For months he had no paper. No books. Not even the smallest comforts. When he was finally allowed to write again, he began a letter to Lord Alfred Douglas that would eventually become *De Profundis*: part indictment, part confession, part soul-searching howl. He no longer wrote with dazzle. He wrote with hunger. "I must learn how to be happy," he wrote, "as I must learn how to walk." This wasn't Wilde the icon anymore. It was Wilde trying to make sense of the wreckage.

He emerged physically broken, bankrupt, and publicly ruined. His name, once a ticket to every room that mattered, had become a punchline and a warning. When he was released in 1897, no crowd waited. No doors reopened. He left England and never returned. Under a pseudonym, he published one last poem. The rest of his life was scattered across borrowed rooms and borrowed names. He was alive, but never visible in the way he had been. Still, he wrote quietly and painfully, refusing to vanish completely.

Wilde didn't die for art. He died because the world decided his honesty was indecency, his beauty an offense, his visibility a threat. Neither was he a martyr. He was a man: funny, reckless, brilliant, arrogant. Wilde made mistakes, lingering long after he should have gone, trusting that the world would protect someone who made it laugh. He also believed that art should shimmer, that love should speak, and that hiding who you are is the slowest kind of death. For a while, he lived that belief out loud.

That's what made him dangerous, and that's what makes him matter. We still live in a world that rewards what's easy to swallow and punishes those who show too much. We tell people to speak up until their truth is inconvenient. We cheer boldness until it asks more of us than applause. Visibility has a cost. It can break something open, but it can also break something free.

Either way, it always has a cost.

They didn't just imprison him. They tried to erase him. His name fell out of conversation, his work slid off the shelves, and theaters stopped reviving his plays. Publishers distanced themselves. Critics who once praised his wit now used it to mock him. Friends disappeared, and acquaintances crossed the street to avoid him. In a single season, he went from darling to pariah.

Even after his release, the stigma clung to him. He wasn't allowed the dignity of obscurity, only the spectacle of public decline. Landlords refused him, employers avoided him, and every door that once opened at his wit now stayed shut. His presence alone could scandalize a room. It was a fall from grace, but more than that, it was an organized forgetting.

After Wilde's death, the silence continued. His plays went unperformed, his essays slipped out of print, and his name remained a warning. Parents used him as a moral fable. Writers avoided quoting him. Schools left him out altogether. When people did speak of him, it was with pity, scorn, or caution. He was recast as a fallen figure, too proud, too flamboyant, too foolish to leave well enough alone. A man who mistook style for substance and paid the price.

It was a way to let the culture off the hook. If Wilde had simply gone too far, there was no need to ask what had actually broken him. If he was the author of his own ruin, then the ruin itself could be ignored. But the words didn't vanish. They crept back through dog-eared books, through whispered quotes, through secondhand copies passed between hands that understood the risk he'd taken. His epigrams returned first, then the essays, then the plays, and at last the man himself.

By then, it was safe. The world could only reclaim Wilde when he was no longer a threat. With his body buried, his voice cut short, and his future gone, the culture finally made room. He could be quoted without being answered and admired without being defended. He was easier as a myth than as a man. His visibility had made people complicit: they laughed, then watched him fall. They printed his lines, then printed his sentence. No one wanted to admit that silence can punish as deeply as words. What he wrote was impossible to erase. It was stylized, subversive, defiantly queer. It spoke to too many people who, like Wilde, had learned that honesty in the wrong room could be treated as a crime.

It's easy to celebrate Wilde now. Quote him in classrooms, print his lines on tote bags, name bars, and bookstores after him. He can be turned into a symbol of wit and style and sharp rejoinders. It's important to remember that Wilde didn't suffer for cleverness. He suffered for visibility. He performed the truth, and when that truth became too inconvenient for the world around him, it wasn't only his career that collapsed. His body collapsed too. His freedom. His future.

So what does it mean to admire Wilde now, in a world where truth still carries consequences? Who still pays that price today? Some are invited in, until the winds of "tolerance" shift. Held up as proof of progress, until they say something uncomfortable. Asked to represent a whole community, until they become difficult to market. Offered a platform, then punished the moment they use it.

Visibility is still offered with an asterisk. You're welcome to be seen, as long as you behave. You might be honored, so long as you stay bland. You can even be out, provided you're not too outspoken. The moment you push past that line, the applause fades and the punishment begins. Who gets punished not for what they did, but for refusing to disappear? Wilde's story isn't a historical footnote. It's a mirror.

You don't have to be a playwright to know what it feels like when your truth is treated as too much. You see it when people shift in their seats the moment you stop editing yourself, when the welcome turns out to be for a smaller version of you, the one who already knew how to shrink. We still ask people to flatten themselves for comfort, and we still punish those who stay three-dimensional. That was Wilde's refusal. It was that refusal, more than his wit, more than his work, more even than his love, that the world wouldn't tolerate.

There are still whole countries where love like his is criminalized, and schools where books like his are banned. Industries still reward spectacle while punishing sincerity. Audiences embrace performance, but the truth behind it rarely earns the same reception. That's why so many people still walk a tightrope between being known and being safe, between saying what they mean and being allowed to stay. It doesn't just happen to artists. It happens to anyone whose existence unsettles the status quo, anyone told they're too much, anyone asked to act right, fit in, be easier to explain. Visibility isn't just being seen. It's being seen and surviving it.

That's why Wilde's story still resonates. He tried to defend himself in court, even to deny what he felt, yet he stayed where everyone could see him and paid the full price for it. Not everyone pays that price so publicly, but the fear of punishment for being real is still with us. Some feel it in classrooms where honesty earns detention. Others feel it in boardrooms where authenticity gets praised in slogans but punished in practice. For many, the stakes are whether they get to keep their job, their safety, or their place in the room.

What about when the cost isn't your livelihood, but your belonging? That moment when the room goes quiet, when the air changes, when the laughter dies not because the joke didn't land but because no one expected it from you. That's a tax too. A tax on tone, on posture, on presence. A tax on being more than what someone else is comfortable with. Wilde paid it in public. Most people pay it quietly, in ways that don't leave a record: the pause in a conversation that hangs heavier than it should, the message that never comes back, the chance that seemed almost certain but never arrives. They pay it in the pressure to laugh at the joke that cuts, to nod at the rule that diminishes, or to keep making themselves acceptable enough to stay in the room.

It still speaks to every artist asked to strip the personal out of their work, to every queer person told to tone it down, to every truth-teller celebrated only until the truth cuts too close. Even now, we praise courage, but mostly when it comes with a tidy ending. We love the rebel who triumphs, the outcast who's finally proven right. What about those who tell the truth and lose for it? What do we do with the stories that don't resolve or with the lives that never get repaired? We downplay them. We say he was brilliant but reckless. We call it tragic but avoidable. We dismiss it as a different time. All of it is easier than admitting we still punish people the same way.

You've probably felt that pressure, though not in a courtroom or a headline. It might happen in a job interview, when you hear yourself answer too directly and see the tension. Or at a family dinner, where you swallow the truth because you know it would sour the evening. Even in a submission call that claimed to want boldness, then sent your work back stamped as "too much." You learn to scan the room, to measure the cost, and to hold something back.

So you tone down the language, rewrite the line, and let the piece land a little quieter or a little more polite. You tell yourself it's strategy, that it's temporary, that it's what survival requires. You know revision can be a way to get closer to the truth, to cut what is sloppy or defensive so the real thing can finally be heard. This doesn't feel like that kind. This time you're editing to soothe someone else, to slip past a gatekeeper who doesn't want to be confronted. Still, there's a part of you that wonders what the first version might have done if you'd let it breathe. The revision still matters, but something gets lost in the trimming, some pulse of honesty that rattled you or them or both. Ever since, the question lingers: was that the part that might have made a difference?

Perhaps that version has lingered with you ever since, the too-bold draft you reshaped just to get through. It might still sit half-formed, tucked in a drawer or lodged in the back of your mind, waiting. You've told yourself you'll return to it when the timing feels safer, when you feel stronger, when the world is more willing to hear it. But what if that's not how it works? What if the risk has to come first?

After all, someone is always watching and waiting for a sign that their own sharp edges don't need to be dulled or that their truth doesn't have to be trimmed out. Maybe they'll never say it and maybe you'll never meet, but your refusal to disappear might be the one thing that finally gives them permission to begin. Visibility draws fire, but it also draws people. The ones who needed to see it happen. The people told to quiet down, to blend in, to play along. The ones still deciding how much of themselves they can risk bringing into the room. Every time you let yourself be seen, you leave a trail behind you. Something someone else can follow when they're ready.

Few people can afford to be bold all at once or to take the same risks. When someone does, when Wilde takes the fall and keeps writing, it shifts the ground for everyone else. It makes space. That's the real legacy: words carrying the courage beneath them, beauty carrying the risk that made it possible. The choice to speak when silence would have been safer. The choice to stay visible, even when it costs everything. Visibility exposes you, but it also makes denial harder.

Because somewhere, someone is watching with the same questions: can you survive it, is it worth it, does it end in exile or in freedom? The harder question is whether your truth can survive performance, disguise, or silence. Wilde understood that. Long before it became legacy, it was a choice. He stepped onto stages and said what the world wasn't ready to hear, not because it was safe to do so, but because it mattered. If no one says it, we all go on pretending it isn't there. It's about knowing the risk of being seen and deciding to show up anyway.

Wilde understood that long before the culture was willing to admit what it had done to him. Visibility cost him nearly everything, but once the truth had been said aloud, the world couldn't make it untrue again.

Frédéric Chopin

There's a story about Chopin being asked to perform in a large concert hall. The setting felt wrong to Frédéric, the air too thick with expectation, the acoustics too wide, and the crowd too hungry for spectacle. He declined. Not rudely. Just quietly. No tantrum or manifesto, no declarations about the state of music. He simply said no thank you.

That kind of refusal doesn't usually get remembered. It doesn't spark movements or show up in the headlines. There's no blood, no exile, no memorable scene. But Chopin's entire life was made of that same quiet instinct: don't play their game or meet them on their terms. Don't deliver what they expect. Still, he gave them something. More than something. Just not in the shape they expected.

When he performed, which wasn't often, it was in private salons, rooms full of velvet and perfume, maybe two dozen people gathered around a small piano, straining to catch every note. His playing was delicate, but not fragile. In Chopin's case, it meant refined down to the exact vibration he wanted to leave behind. One listener said it was like watching someone reveal a secret. Another compared it to prayer. He hated raising his voice, in conversation or in music. The full force of an orchestra wasn't something he needed or even wanted. He composed as if holding his breath for intimacy's sake. To be heard clearly in a room full of shouting, sometimes the best thing you can do is whisper.

His temperament was nothing like Caravaggio's rage or Wilde's spectacle. Chopin never aimed to shock. Instead, he whispered into the center of a century obsessed with bombast. Where others turned to opera and grand symphonies, Chopin wrote short forms: preludes, nocturnes, études that lasted only a few minutes but said more than most hour-long scores. He avoided the public stage, gave recitals only in private homes, and performed like he was letting you in on a secret. Even the way he sat at the piano, with shoulders curved, head bowed, and barely moving, felt like an invitation to lean closer. It was a form, a refusal turned into an aesthetic.

Maybe the most subversive thing of all was that it worked. Chopin became essential by staying quiet. He was revered without ever demanding it. He left the pursuit of celebrity to others and kept to his own company. His music sounded like memory, something already disappearing, and yet it lingered. Instead of aiming for volume or spectacle, he wrote to be the note you couldn't forget.

Chopin left Poland at twenty and never came back. He left for a tour that wasn't meant to be permanent. He had a suitcase, some concert dates, and a letter of introduction to a few musicians in Vienna. Then the November Uprising broke out. Polish rebels rose against Russian occupation, and the crackdown that followed was brutal. When the smoke cleared, Poland was no longer the country Chopin had known. The tsar's regime tightened, and dissent grew dangerous. For Chopin, exile became the only real hope of safety.

His friends begged him to come back and join the resistance or to write music to support the cause. He didn't, at least not publicly. He wasn't a revolutionary in that way. His rebellion was slower, stranger, more internal. While he was composing in drawing rooms and private salons, others were marching, fighting, and dying. Guilt threaded through his letters. He raised money and grieved from a distance, all while continuing to compose.

He made his way to Paris, where the salons were glittering, the pianos plentiful, and no one expected a sickly émigré to carry the weight of a fallen homeland. But he did anyway. His mazurkas and polonaises, Polish dance forms, became vessels for a kind of hidden homesickness. They weren't nostalgic in the simple sense. They were uneasy, with rhythms that skipped and hesitated, and melodies that seemed to search for something already lost.

In his first months in Paris, Chopin wandered the streets alone, unsure if he would stay. He was twenty-one now, and his French was fluent but accented. He had no home, no patrons, and no clear future. He wrote to a friend that he felt like a ghost, present but unrecognizable. That winter, he played a handful of salons, then collapsed for days, too ill to get out of bed. One night, caught in the rain with no carriage and nowhere to go, he ducked into a church and sat in the back row until morning.

Paris would eventually revere him, but at first, it barely noticed him. He began to write his first Parisian works, sketches of preludes and etudes, pieces that sound now like someone learning how to speak in a new language, carefully, note by note. He never explained this, perhaps because he didn't need to. One listener said his music sounded like someone weeping for their country. That may have been projection, but it doesn't feel wrong. His Poland was a ghost and he carried it in every line. Exile may not have turned Chopin into a radical, but it made his music sharply precise. I always hear it in the silences, in the way his music holds back, hovers on a single phrase, then breaks it like glass. The grief lived deeper than just the theatrical, pressed into every note by what can't be said aloud.

He gave only a handful of public concerts during his entire life. What mattered to Chopin wasn't being seen, it was being heard. More than anything, he longed for home. In his final months, when his lungs were failing and even walking across a room left him gasping, he made one last request: that when he died, his heart be returned to Warsaw. After his funeral in Paris, his sister smuggled it back across the border in a jar of cognac, hidden under her skirt. It was buried in a church pillar beneath a plaque that reads, simply, "Where your treasure is, there will your heart be also." His body remained in France, but his heart made the journey home.

His fragility isn't the whole story, but it's a big part of it. Chopin was ill most of his adult life. He coughed blood, shivered in warm rooms, and tired easily. His hands trembled, and his lungs felt like they belonged to someone else. There's a debate about what he suffered from. Tuberculosis is the most likely answer, but some biographers suggest cystic fibrosis, epilepsy, or chronic bronchitis layered with anxiety. Whatever the diagnosis, the fact is he was always unwell, and he kept going anyway. The world around him didn't know what to do with that. The Romantic ideal was vigor, intensity, and bravado. Chopin gave them none of it. He played with his head bowed and his eyes closed, as if the piano were something sacred he didn't want to disturb too much. He hated being stared at while he performed and hated the pressure to be dazzling. He didn't mind being admired, but he wanted to earn it on the page, not by force of charisma.

He avoided concert halls because they cost him too much. The pounding force of public attention, the roar of large venues, the physical toll of performance: he couldn't sustain it, so he didn't try. Instead, he built a world scaled to his body. He played in rooms small enough to hear him breathe. He taught and composed, honing an aesthetic that demanded, above all else, closeness. At one of his few formal concerts, a rare public appearance in Paris, he played with such softness that audience members in the back strained to hear. A critic called it "introverted to the point of vanishing." Those who sat close described it very differently. They said it felt like eavesdropping on something holy, as if he weren't performing at them but simply allowing them to overhear. One woman wept without knowing why. Someone else called it the most personal sound they'd ever heard in a room full of strangers.

That was Chopin's refusal. He never tried to fill the room with noise. Instead, he drew listeners close, inviting them to hush and lean in. He turned performance into intimacy and made the world come closer. Some critics read his restraint as weakness. They wanted him to be like Liszt: fiery, demonstrative, overflowing. But Liszt was his friend, not his role model. Chopin's power was in clarity. He could devastate with four bars, not by dazzling but by drawing you in.

His hands were small, so he redefined what virtuosity could be. His health was unreliable, so he treated energy like currency, spending it only where it mattered most. He poured intimacy into his music, letting it speak on his behalf. Delicacy became a kind of armor. He made it impossible to separate his physical limits from his artistic choices because he learned to work with illness rather than against it. He wrote like someone who didn't have time to waste on things that didn't matter.

This wasn't a competition with the Liszts and Berliozes of his time, with their orchestral bombast and wild public personas. While they thundered across Europe, Chopin made something quieter, finer, and impossible to imitate. He was deliberate and that was the difference.

It would've been easy to overlook him. In an era obsessed with spectacle, Chopin chose a scale so small it bordered on private. There were no operas or symphonies in his catalogue, no grand masses or programmatic spectacles. He wrote for one instrument: his own, and he made it vast. That was a challenge to the very idea of what counted as serious music. Opera was treated as the apex, and orchestral works as the true test of a composer's muscle. The bigger the better, the louder the more legitimate. Chopin didn't play that game. He took the most familiar instrument in Europe and transformed it into a world unto itself.

Before Chopin, the piano was versatile but limited. It filled parlors and accompanied singers. It kept students busy. In his hands, it became mythic. He didn't expand its range; he deepened its soul. Every emotion lived there: rage, reverence, restraint. There was no need to add more instruments. The piano was enough because he made it enough.

He didn't invent the étude, but Chopin was the one who turned those technical exercises into something poetic. What others used as dry drills, he transformed into miniature dramas that demanded both speed and feeling. The same went for his nocturnes. He made the night feel like a story, not just a setting. Even his waltzes subvert expectation. They glide but sometimes stumble, pausing for long moments before rushing ahead, as if the music itself is uncertain about where it wants to go. That tension between grace and doubt is what makes them linger. And the mazurkas: on the surface, they're simple Polish dances, but Chopin twisted them, shifted the accents, bent the rhythm, added dissonance where ease would've been simpler. He turned folk forms into psychological landscapes and embedded exile into structure.

These were radical moves, even if no one called them that at the time. He avoided essays about his methods and never debated them in salons. He rarely published commentary of any kind. He just kept composing, and what he composed whispered something no one had heard before.

His refusal to go big was intentional. It was clarity. He didn't need an orchestra to shake a listener or a stage to create awe. He could do it with a single chord held too long, a trill that refused to resolve, a cadence that dissolved instead of ending. This was precision, not minimalism. The kind of restraint that comes from discipline. It's easy to mistake the miniature for the minor, but Chopin's small forms held galaxies. He just needed a piano, a room, and the right kind of silence.

The closest thing Chopin had to stability was George Sand. She was everything he wasn't: outspoken, physically robust, socially fearless. She dressed in men's clothes because it gave her freedom. She smoked cigars, wrote under a male pseudonym, and commanded rooms in a way Chopin never could. Where he shrank from the public gaze, she met it head-on. Where he withdrew, she advanced. They seemed destined to clash, and eventually they did. For a time, though, they built something that worked.

They spent nine years together writing, wintering, and hosting. In her country estate, Nohant, Chopin composed some of his most intimate and enduring work: the Barcarolle, the B minor Sonata, the haunting late mazurkas. In the winter of 1838, they traveled to Mallorca, hoping the climate would help his lungs, but it rained constantly, and the monastery they rented was cold, damp, and full of echo. Locals grew suspicious of them: Sand in trousers, Chopin coughing blood. Pharmacies refused to fill his prescriptions. The piano they'd arranged for arrived broken. He wrote anyway, scribbling drafts of the Preludes on damp manuscript paper as his fever climbed.

Sand kept the household together, handling the cooking and the children, while Chopin grew quieter and more withdrawn. In her letters, she described him as both angelic and maddening. "He is dying," she wrote once, "and I am exhausted." They left the island early, both changed. Chopin brought back sketches of pieces that would become some of his most enduring work, but something between them had cracked. Chopin's health was a constant negotiation. Sand often became his caretaker, managing his moods and fevers while also managing her household, children, and career. Eventually, the imbalance wore them both down. What began in admiration soured into resentment. She accused him of being cold, passive, impossible to reach, and he withdrew even further. Letters stopped, and when they separated she never spoke to him again.

But what they made during those years mattered. It was more than the art itself; it was the way they redefined what it meant to create under pressure. Chopin never tried to outpace death or pretend it wasn't hovering nearby. He allowed it in, working with that presence always in the room. The music from this period is pared down, essential, like someone finished with explanations, speaking only what matters. Fragility in his late work was a reality. The music grew from suffering, rooted and persistent. Chopin composed not to prove endurance, but because endurance was all that remained.

There's no myth of triumph here. He didn't recover or rise again; he simply faded. Yet as his body failed, his attention grew sharper. Those late pieces are quiet, sometimes strange, sometimes left unfinished. They sound less like performance than breath itself, or the hush that follows. For Chopin, limit was a frame. He shaped the work to fit what was possible. This was a kind of vision, choosing depth over display.

At the time of his death, not everyone agreed that Chopin mattered. Some critics dismissed his work as salon music: elegant, yes, but unserious, too delicate and decorative, too closely associated with women and amateurs to belong in the canon of great composers. Others found him too emotional, not masculine enough, not rigorous enough, not loud enough to last. But the thing about quiet resistance is that it doesn't announce itself. It embeds and waits, then slowly starts to shift the foundation under everything else.

That shift is clear from his impact. Chopin changed what the piano was for. He taught generations of pianists that the goal wasn't power, it was control, that what mattered wasn't volume but voice. After him, no one could write for the instrument without hearing his influence. Even the composers who sought to rebel against him couldn't help echoing him in the process.

His technical innovations included rubato, inner voicing, and unexpected modulations. Over time, they became part of the standard vocabulary. His forms served as blueprints, and his sound, once dismissed as too delicate, became aspirational. By the time Ravel and Debussy arrived, they were building directly on the ground he had already broken for them. Even Liszt, who once outshouted everyone, came to revere Chopin's restraint as a kind of genius he couldn't replicate.

Yet Chopin didn't seek legacy. He didn't expect it, and he never tried to dominate a movement or leave a school of thought behind him. There were no students of note, no manifestos, no grand finale. He didn't even orchestrate his own funeral. It was Sand, and his friends, and his sister who made sure the music was played, the heart was buried, and the myth set in motion. It's a radical kind of exit to make something so enduring without ever insisting on it, to shape the future through presence alone.

There's a piece he wrote not long before he died: unfinished, unpublished, a mazurka in F minor. It drifts more than it dances. The phrases hesitate, repeat, and eventually dissolve. It's barely there, with no big ending, just a quiet, fractured farewell. He never revised or performed it, but it still made its way into the world, posthumously and quietly. Now it's played in recitals, studied, wept over.

This is what his refusal looked like at the end. One small, incomplete, unforgettable gesture. His music barely raised its voice, yet it outlived revolution, exile, sickness, heartbreak, and nearly two centuries of people insisting he should've been louder. He made intimacy sound like power, and he made fragility unforgettable.

He closes our section on refusal because his is a much less common kind, but one you may still recognize. If you've ever been told to take up more space, to speak up, pitch harder, make it big, or don't bother, Chopin's for you. Wilde was punished for being too much; Chopin was punished for being too little. The point isn't that the right posture saves you, only that the game is rigged either way. Revising yourself to fit in is the trap. If your refusal isn't the kind people notice, if it doesn't look like confrontation or rebellion or defiance on stage, it still counts. Quiet is not cowardly and soft is not the same as small. There's a kind of persistence that never gets applause. It doesn't come with slogans or a crowd to cheer it on. That persistence can be almost invisible. It's the choice to keep going when no one expects it, to keep making your way when it feels like no one's watching, to keep your own pace in a world that demands performance.

It can be lonely to create without making a big splash. Not making a scene, staying in the background while others announce themselves. It's easy to wonder if you're doing it wrong, if quiet means forgettable, if the world will ever hear what you're trying to say. Chopin never tried to win over the world by force. What mattered was exactness, control, and the refusal to mistake scale for seriousness. He entered it quietly, as if asking a question, and left it changed. He never crashed gates or rewrote the rules through shock or spectacle. Instead, he played a quiet revolution in a borrowed room and trusted it would carry through time. Louder wasn't the thing. Some work doesn't conquer the room. It alters the ear.

Chopin never mistook volume for power. He barely performed, published little, certainly never shouted, and still his music changed everything. What could seem slight in scale held enormous emotional gravity because he honed the music until every gesture carried weight. He didn't live to see how fully the world would come back to him.

The Price Tag of Vision

Every big idea comes with a bill and paying it will usually cost you more than money.

PABLO PICASSO | JAMES BALDWIN | FRANCISCO GOYA | MARY SHELLEY

Pablo Picasso

There's no shortage of quotes from Picasso. He made sure of that. "I don't search," he said. "I find." He claimed art was a lie that made us see the truth. He compared himself to God. He called women "machines for suffering." He insisted that every act of creation was first an act of destruction. He was blunt, brilliant, theatrical, and cruel, and he wanted you to know it. He's still the most famous artist of the twentieth century. Picasso stands for genius, innovation, and power. His reputation's so big it almost loses its shape, drifting into a myth that hovers above everything else.

The art world celebrated his ego, and his charisma became part of the work. Even his control, womanizing, and violence got folded into the myth and rebranded as creative fuel. Biographers labeled him complicated, critics saw a force of nature, and museums called him essential, but for the women who tried to survive and eventually broke beside him, he wasn't a myth. He was a man, and not a gentle one.

This chapter doesn't start with the paintings, the movements he led, or the eras he changed. It starts with the fact that we've built a whole language to let certain men behave however they want, as long as they make something we decide is worth it. We talk about genius like it's something you can't question, but genius is just a story we tell, and like most stories, it protects the people with the most power.

Picasso certainly had power, and he used it. In his art, in his relationships, in the way he moved through the world. The question isn't whether he made extraordinary work. He did. The question is what got ignored, excused, or erased to make room for it, and who's still paying that price? Throughout Picasso's life, the pattern kept repeating. He met young women, often teenagers, flattered and isolated them, and turned them into his muses. He painted, controlled, and eventually replaced them, sometimes with someone even younger. He called this inspiration and history called it a creative phase. If we're honest about it now, it would be most accurately called a pattern of harm.

There was Fernande, who helped him survive his Blue Period and nearly died of hunger doing it. There was Eva, who withered and died of illness while he painted canvases declaring his love, but he disappeared from her bedside. There was Olga, his first wife, a ballerina from the Ballets Russes, whose image he twisted and distorted as their marriage unraveled. There was Marie-Thérèse, a teenager when they met, whom he kept hidden for years while she bore his child and waited for him to choose a life with her. He never did.

There was Dora Maar, a brilliant artist in her own right, often remembered only as "the weeping woman." Picasso photographed her tears, painted them, distorted them into grotesque abstraction, then told friends that women "are machines for suffering," and Dora was "the perfect example." She suffered a nervous breakdown after their breakup and underwent years of electroshock therapy. He described it as part of her "artistic temperament."

Then there was Jacqueline Roque, who stayed with him until his death. He painted her more than any other woman. He also controlled her completely. After he died, she barred many of his children and former lovers from the funeral. Years later, she took her own life. Two of Picasso's lovers killed themselves. So did one of his grandsons. Others suffered breakdowns, illnesses, and lifelong trauma. Through it all, Picasso kept painting. Kept rising. Kept being called a genius. Not despite the damage, but with it written directly into the work. He knew exactly how he was seen, and he cultivated it. "I am not a great artist," he once said. "I am a public entertainer who has understood his time." That wasn't how the art world treated him. They called him a visionary. A magician. A genius. That word, "genius," has always had a way of making people want to look the other way.

It wasn't just that Picasso made extraordinary work. It was that the work seemed to excuse everything else. The cruelty, the infidelity, the possessiveness, the predation: every part of it was folded into the myth. He was difficult, people said, but brilliant. Complicated, but important. He was a man of appetites, a force of nature, a chaos others learned to excuse. It wasn't just tolerated, it was romanticized. Critics praised his "artistic hunger" without naming what he consumed. Museums exalted his portraits without questioning who got erased in the process. Even now, his biographers often describe his lovers only as muses, his betrayals as drama, and his violence as passion. When Marie-Thérèse tried to take her life after their breakup, Picasso's comment was, "She almost killed herself. I had to hide all the ropes." He told the story like it was a joke.

We built whole systems to indulge it. Across publishing, film, and museums, great work often reclassifies harm as collateral. The tormented genius story stretches to cover almost any injury, so long as the output keeps coming. The draw isn't just power; it's proximity. People want to stand close to greatness, to touch it, to benefit from it. Dealers, curators, and collectors keep the artist mythic because the story sells. When the facts complicate that sale, they edit the truth. The genius defense works because it flatters everyone involved. Excuse Picasso, and you share in his importance. Protect him, promote him, exhibit him, sell him, and some of that glow lands on you. You aren't just making money, which is hard enough in this business. You're making history. And history resists being questioned.

Picasso once said, "Painting is not made to decorate apartments. It is an instrument of war." In *Guernica*, that line held true. Painted after the bombing of a Basque village during the Spanish Civil War, the canvas is jagged and haunted. Faces twist in terror, the horse screams, and a lightbulb glares like a godless eye. There is neither hero nor redemption, only rupture. Yet, for all its political power, *Guernica* is an outlier in Picasso's body of work. Most of his output wasn't aimed outward. It turned inward, toward the women in his life, the lovers he claimed, and the muses he consumed. Over and over, the work reveals his fixation with control: bodies distorted, rearranged, split open, and reassembled. It was called innovation. It was called Cubism. What if it was also a kind of domination? Like a way to fracture the women he couldn't fully possess.

He painted Dora Maar with hands like claws, eyes like shattered glass, tears sharp as razors. She was a surrealist photographer before she met him. Afterward, she was best known as his Weeping Woman. She once said, "All the portraits of me are lies. They're Picassos. Not one is Dora Maar." When he was done with her, she had a breakdown. He moved on. He met Marie-Thérèse when she was seventeen. He was forty-five. He didn't just paint her; he displayed her. In swelling curves, pastel nudes, soft limbs parted and pulled toward him. The art world praised their intimacy. It rarely paused to name the power imbalance. Years later, she hanged herself in their shared home. His final partner, Jacqueline Roque, was painted more than 400 times.

None of this erases the work's importance, but it does change how we should see it. The genius myth insists the art stands apart from the life, untouched by anything beyond the canvas. In reality, the story lives in the paint. His portraits of women weren't just breakthroughs in style; they were acts of possession. When he distorted a face, it didn't always open up new possibilities. Sometimes it was about control, about holding on to someone who was slipping away. We either missed that, or we didn't want to see it. In fact, we cheered him for it.

There's a long list of names orbiting Picasso's: Olga, Dora, Françoise, Marie-Thérèse, Jacqueline. Most people know them only in relation to him. Muses. Models. Lovers. But many were artists themselves: some painters, some photographers, some writers. Their work was diminished, dismissed, or simply absorbed into his mythology. In some cases, he erased them completely.

Dora Maar was already a prominent surrealist when they met. She was making strange, experimental photographs: distorted reflections, unsettling juxtapositions, what I would call early visual poetry. She was friends with André Breton, and she had her own exhibitions. After Picasso, her work was recast as a side effect of proximity. He claimed to have "saved her" from surrealism. What actually happened was that she stopped making work for years after their breakup. He said she went mad. She said he broke her. The evidence in the public record suggests her telling is more credible than his.

Marie-Thérèse Walter wasn't given the chance to be anything but a muse. Her life after him was quieter, but no less tragic. She gave him a child. She appeared in some of his most sensual, celebrated paintings. After he died, she also ended her life with a rope. But in retrospectives, she remains a soft pastel blur, one of his "great inspirations," rarely named as someone who might have had her own ambitions or her own voice.

Françoise Gilot did have a voice, and she was one of the few who refused to let him silence it. She was an accomplished painter, decades younger than Picasso. She outlived him by nearly fifty years. Her memoir, *Life with Picasso*, became a rare counter-narrative. In it, she described his cruelty, his manipulations, his fear of aging, his contempt for women who stopped being pliant. Picasso tried to block the book's publication. When he failed, he tried to block her career. That worked better. Galleries pulled back. Critics questioned her motives. She kept painting anyway.

Jacqueline Roque stayed with him the longest. After his death, she became the gatekeeper of his estate, and in many ways, of his myth. She was intensely protective, sometimes vindictive. Her suicide was the second among his partners. People whispered about it, but no one dared to rewrite the narrative by then.

The genius myth centralizes one figure so completely that everyone else becomes a footnote. It doesn't ask what these women might have created if their work had been seen on its own terms. It doesn't question how many others were pushed out of the room to make more space for him. It accepts the orbit as natural. In doing so, it casts his gravity as unavoidable, but it wasn't. It was chosen, maintained, curated, and sold. The genius myth needed casualties, and it got plenty of them. The people who benefited from Picasso weren't just the dealers and critics who championed him. They were the institutions, the historians, the curators, and even the culture at large, anyone who had a stake in selling the idea that greatness justifies damage. He didn't build the myth alone. He just embodied it so fully that it became almost impossible to question without shaking the foundations of modern art itself.

His dealers loved him because he sold. His volatility, his affairs, even his cruelty, all of it made him more valuable, not less. There was always a new phase, a new lover, a new transformation to chart. His life became a marketing engine: the more he disrupted, the more it seemed to confirm his brilliance. Galleries competed for the right to exhibit him. Museums centered him in their narratives. Scholars wrote volumes to explain his every shift. When someone pointed out the wreckage he left behind, the answer was always the same: yes but look at the work. The work is extraordinary.

That's what makes this so hard. You can't explain him away, or argue that he wasn't important. But importance alone shouldn't confer immunity. Picasso's story gets used as evidence that genius needs room. Interference is cast as dangerous and if the cost is broken people, so be it. Let's be clear: He destroyed women, and we called it inspiration. He consumed, and we called it evolution. The market rewarded this, so did the institutions, and so did the stories we told about him. He became the blueprint, not just for how to be great, but for what greatness was allowed to excuse. For over a century, that idea has echoed outward, influencing how we treat talented artists.

The most lasting damage may have been to the idea of accountability itself because if Picasso can do anything and still be a genius, what happens when the next artist tries? And when the next man in power follows suit? Which behaviors get waved away because we've been trained to believe that certain people, certain talents, are enough to offset or excuse the harm they cause? The genius myth protects the gifted while endangering everyone else. If this doesn't already feel like enough to justify a reckoning with his legacy, don't forget that the damage wasn't limited to the women. Yes, they bore the brunt of his cruelty, but Picasso's wake was wider than that. There were children, colleagues, rivals, imitators, and, less obviously, the generation of artists and thinkers who absorbed his behavior as part of the genius package.

Picasso modeled a way of working that treated harm as a reasonable side effect of vision. He did it so publicly, with so much backing from the institutions around him, it became something bigger than a pattern. It created permission. When someone like Picasso is declared essential, the institutions that benefit from his status become invested in that story. Museums, galleries, critics, collectors, whole ecosystems rise around the myth of greatness. And when the myth gets tangled up with harm, the harm often gets quietly folded into the story as part of the price. Not just the price he paid to make it, but the price we're supposed to accept on behalf of everyone else. This is what happens when we reward only the loudest voices. Success starts to look like absolution. History can look like something built on the assumption that the work must be protected at all costs, especially from the truth.

The cost was built into the very structure of the art world. Every time Picasso was elevated, someone else got pushed aside. Galleries gave him another wall, critics announced he was the future, patrons threw money at his latest experiment, and others were left scrambling for space. With support like that, Picasso did more than dominate movements; he consumed them. He laid claim to Cubism, Primitivism, and Expressionism, often by absorbing the work of others and amplifying it with institutional power. Georges Braque, without whom Cubism wouldn't exist, was reduced to a supporting role in his own movement. African artists, whose masks and sculptures inspired some of Picasso's most famous pieces, went uncredited and unnamed. None of this was unique to him. No art happens in a vacuum; artists are always borrowing, answering, and transforming what came before. The difference in Picasso's case was the scale of the reward and the way the story narrowed around his name while everyone else stayed invisible. He became the most rewarded example of this pattern, which made it easier for everyone else to follow his lead.

We like to believe that genius rises on its own. That brilliance is self-evident. It's a good story. Aspirational. The truth is that attention is curated, legacy is constructed, and when we celebrate people like Picasso without interrogating how they got to the center, who helped, who looked away, and who paid the price, it reinforces a hierarchy where the same kinds of people get elevated and the same kinds of people get erased. Once that dynamic is established, it replicates itself. Picasso made protection look like part of the deal. Cruelty was reframed as charisma. Affairs were praised as artistic fuel. Dominance was cast as inevitability. That became the industry's "shining example," not only for how to be an artist but for how to be a man in the arts.

Think about how many filmmakers, writers, painters, musicians, and directors have been excused, elevated, and defended because we've been taught that brilliance is rare and must be preserved at all costs. Think, too, about how often the people they harmed were dismissed, doubted, or ignored. It certainly didn't start with Picasso, but he made the formula famous.

What's left out of those stories is the cost. Not just to the people closest to harm, but to the work itself. What never gets made when cruelty is considered normal? What gets lost when so many people are told, one way or another, that the space isn't for them? We lose more than we think when we reward only the most dominant voice. The subtle and the strange slip away. Collaboration and care vanish with them. Art that refuses to shout goes unheard. Artists who won't step on others just to be noticed fade from view. Something even deeper vanishes too: our ability to imagine creative greatness as something that doesn't require destruction.

The Picasso myth is seductive. The genius who changed everything, who lived for art, who couldn't be tamed, but myths are almost always shaped by what they leave out. This one leaves out a truth we can't afford to keep ignoring, if we keep excusing harm in the name of brilliance, we're not just failing to hold people accountable. We're narrowing the future of art to something meaner, smaller, and more familiar than it needs to be. The work was great, yes, but not because of the damage. The longer we pretend otherwise, the longer we keep telling the next generation that harm is a cost worth paying, as long as you make something great.

We can do better, but only if we stop mistaking legacy for permission. It still matters because we're still making excuses. Picasso is everywhere, on dorm room posters, in doctor's offices, across books, documentaries, retrospectives, and all sorts of merchandise. You may have noticed that he's even in the book you're reading right now. His name itself became a shorthand for brilliance, so common it turned into metaphor: the Picasso of finance, the Picasso of baseball. The phrase signals the same thing every time, wild yet great, unruly yet necessary, and, above all, allowed.

Unfortunately, Picasso blurred the line between admiration and permission. Many people stopped trying to draw that line at all. Conversations about flawed geniuses became an easy excuse, as if genius canceled out everything else. Personal turmoil was brushed aside. The paintings still went up on the wall, and the art world kept avoiding the harder questions about what it was built on. When you start asking what gets excused in the name of genius, the whole system feels less steady. This makes lots of people nervous.

Yet the questions are coming, louder than they used to be. Not just about Picasso, but about the entire infrastructure of reverence and reward. Who gets centered, who ends up protected, who finds their image replicated. Younger artists are asking. So are students, critics, curators, and former insiders tired of pretending that brilliance and harm must always be a matched set.

It's uncomfortable, especially for those who loved the work first and only later learned the story behind it. The art still moves them. It still matters. They don't want to throw it out, but they also don't want to ignore the cost. That's the tension, and it's not theoretical. It lives in museum collections, in canon lists, in publishing contracts and gallery shows and boardroom decisions. It lives in every conversation about whose work gets preserved, promoted, and taught.

None of this means we have to stop looking at Picasso. It means we look at him differently, not just as an origin point, or a standard, or a badge of artistic legitimacy, but as a test. What are we willing to see clearly, and what are we still excusing? Why do we keep doing it? We're allowed to admire the work, but we should also ask what that admiration has protected, and what it's erased. If Picasso taught us anything, it's that revolution doesn't require reverence. The formal breakthroughs, including abstraction, distortion, and the fracturing of space, weren't his alone. They were part of a wider movement, a chorus of artists questioning representation, loosening form, and making the invisible visible. But history only had room for one name at the center, and he made sure it was his.

So, let's make more room.

We could start with Georges Braque, the quieter, steadier half of Cubism's origin story. He painted alongside Picasso, often indistinguishably, during the most innovative years of the movement. He didn't chase fame or declare himself a genius; he just kept working. Cubism wouldn't exist without him, and without Cubism, neither would the modern visual vocabulary we now take for granted. Still, most people don't know his name.

Or Sonia Delaunay, who fused color, movement, and abstraction in ways that pushed beyond even what Picasso imagined. Her work was electric, spanning clothing, books, murals, paintings, and stage designs. She wouldn't confine her practice to one form, and she wouldn't separate art from life. Public spaces pulsed with her color long before it was fashionable. Yet, for decades, her contributions were treated as footnotes to her husband Robert's work.

Or Lee Krasner, a fierce, brilliant painter who stood beside Jackson Pollock, then, outworked him, outlived him, and made some of her best work in the years after his death. For decades, critics who should've known better still called her "Mrs. Pollock." She kept painting anyway. Her canvases didn't echo his; they expanded on everything Abstract Expressionism was supposed to be.

There's also Gabriele Münter, María Blanchard, Emily Carr, and Alma Thomas, artists who broke form, reshaped vision, and kept creating even when the spotlight passed them by or never found them at all. The point isn't to replace one myth with another; it's to stop treating genius like a crown that only fits a few heads. Breakthroughs we credit to singular men were often shared, developed in dialogue, or outright stolen. Genius is rarely solitary, but the story of it has too often been.

Let's tell a better story. Most of us won't have dealers, critics, or institutions standing by to protect us. That doesn't make the work less vital. It means we can't confuse recognition with value. The artists who matter most are usually the ones who keep working when nobody's watching, finding ways to create and connect anyway. The art that survives isn't always the art that's initially celebrated. Sometimes it slips through the cracks while the mythmakers are busy protecting the artist they've already built the room around. Picasso's story should make power less impressive and leave us less willing to confuse damage with greatness.

James Baldwin

James Baldwin told the truth too well to be forgiven for it.

He asked for honesty. Demanded it. The clearer he saw the country he loved, the more it treated him as a threat. His voice, celebrated at first, became dangerous the moment it stopped making people feel good. That's what happens when you stop pulling your punches. You end up alone, staring at the bridge you just burned, watching the people on the other side act like you were always the problem, not the one who built it in the first place.

He left because staying meant swallowing himself. Paris was a last-ditch attempt to stay alive, to stay creative, to stay human in a country that only wanted him as long as he didn't speak too loudly, or love too freely, or ask too many questions about whose freedom we were really celebrating. Exile wasn't a choice to escape but a choice to survive, the only way left to keep his voice intact.

He arrived in Paris in 1948 with forty bucks and the memories of too many close calls. He'd been arrested for stealing a sheet from a cheap hotel. He'd tried and failed to live as a writer in Greenwich Village, worked every kind of job that paid just enough to keep him hungry, and buried his best friend the year before. America had shown him, again and again, that it might be willing to read his words but not to accept the fullness of who he was. He was Black, he was gay, he was broke, and he refused to bow his head. That made him a problem no one wanted to solve.

In Paris, he wrote. More than that, he finally breathed. He began to shed the performance of endurance that survival in America had required. "Once you find yourself in another civilization," he wrote, "you're forced to examine your own." From the other side of the ocean, things sharpened. Distance stripped away every excuse. The truths stopped asking for permission and just arrived. *Go Tell It on the Mountain* emerged from that exile. So did *Giovanni's Room*, *The Fire Next Time*, *No Name in the Street*, and *If Beale Street Could Talk*. But the clarity came at a cost. The more deeply Baldwin understood America, the harder it became for him to belong anywhere.

He was famous by thirty. On the cover of *Time* by forty. Admired by the civil rights leaders who carefully overlooked his sexuality and feared by the government that tracked his movements. He sat with Malcolm, walked the streets with Martin, argued late into the night with his friend Lorraine Hansberry, the playwright behind *A Raisin in the Sun*, and watched his words get twisted in the papers. He never relented, even when it would have smoothed his path. Even when it might have made him easier to publish or promote. The more urgent his voice became, the more people tried to turn the volume down. That's the Baldwin we don't often talk about: not just the brilliance, but the isolation that followed. The work changed minds, but it also cost him nearly everything.

From Paris and the south of France, he saw his country more clearly than it saw itself. He saw how the promises of democracy were built on exclusions, how freedom was always qualified, how whiteness in America wasn't just an identity but a shield. "I love America more than any other country in the world," he wrote, "and, exactly for this reason, I insist on the right to criticize her perpetually." That love was never simple. Baldwin wrote as someone who'd been promised belonging and then denied it, someone who had to carve space for himself out of language when the country gave him none. His early success only served to raise the stakes. The more visible he became, the more urgently people wanted him to seem grateful.

His essays were just as unnerving as they were masterful. *The Fire Next Time* didn't offer solutions. It held up a mirror. Many readers, especially white ones, were searching for reassurance instead of reflection. They hoped for inspiration rather than guilt, Baldwin's witness stripped of his judgment. He gave them neither. He refused to pretend that racism was a regional problem, or a thing of the past, or something that would eventually work itself out. He'd never treat sexuality as shameful. He refused to position himself as exceptional, as proof that the system could work if you just worked hard enough. Baldwin was chronicling a country still at war with itself, and with him. He had no interest in survival stories that let people off the hook.

The backlash built over the years and then broke open furiously. As the civil rights era gave way to the Black Power movement, Baldwin's position grew more precarious, whether he was in New York for a debate or back in France trying to write. Too moderate for some, too uncompromising for others. Publishers hesitated. Critics shifted. The literary world, once eager to claim him, began to look elsewhere. The same man who once sat across from Bobby Kennedy, arguing for the lives of Black children in Harlem, found himself pushed to the margins of the national conversation.

He didn't stop writing, but by the early 1970s, his audience had shrunk. He was spending much of his time in France, away from American television studios and lecture halls, and that distance didn't help. But geography wasn't the only reason the room got quieter. The essays grew sharper, more prophetic, and harder for some to swallow. *No Name in the Street*, published in 1972, was messy and brilliant and full of grief. It was also largely ignored, especially by white liberals. Baldwin had outgrown palatability. He no longer wrote to make himself easy to hear. That's what separates him from the writer myths. His rise was never smooth. The public didn't greet him with open arms. His career wandered off the path of success and straight into the kind of trouble that clarity invites. That's what makes his story so urgent now. We're still demanding that entire communities trade truth for belonging.

For his own part, he never stopped being clear, he just stopped being heard. Or maybe it's more accurate to say he stopped being welcomed. The later years were brutal for that reason. Baldwin was too famous and too brilliant to be dismissed outright, so what came instead was erosion. Invitations thinned. Reviews cooled. Getting an essay placed was harder each time. America hadn't turned its back on Baldwin, it had simply lost interest in being challenged. He'd spent so long translating rage into grace, turning complexity into music, that people began to mistake him for something he wasn't. He wasn't there to save anyone. He was there to testify, and the truth he told didn't lose urgency once the marches ended. It only grew heavier. The world shifted. The public moved on, and Baldwin was left with a burden no one else wanted to name.

Friends tried to coax him back into favor. James, just write something like *Notes of a Native Son* again. Go back to what made you famous. Like he could forget what he knew. Like urgency could ever be boxed up and put away. He refused. "The world is held together, really it is, held together, by the love and the passion of a very few people," he wrote near the end of his life. He still believed that, but he also knew exactly how much that belief cost him.

He moved back to France full-time in the 1980s, settling in a small village in Provence. The house was quiet, his circle smaller. Friends were gone. Lovers too. Readers had stopped searching for his name. He wrote anyway, but the work was darker now, jagged, uninterested in pleasing. He knew what had happened. He'd spoken too clearly for too long. The country that once called him its conscience now treated him like a relic. Yet his clarity never dimmed. Reaganism, to Baldwin, was a return to American forgetting, a gloss laid over violence, a tightening of hierarchy. He called it out in real time, even as his audience dwindled. The silence of the well-meaning, he warned, could be as deadly as open hatred. Nothing would change, he said, until we looked directly at what we'd done, and most people would do anything not to look.

Legacy didn't shield him. He pushed back, even when it cost him nearly everyone who once claimed to love his work. He spoke with the same fire, even when it burned him. The work was a burden he couldn't set down. He kept naming what needed to be named, long after the applause stopped. By then, fatigue met him at every turn. The conversations he'd spent his life demanding had grown unbearable for the very audiences that once praised him. He was called bitter, dismissed as out of touch. Critics said he'd become more activist than artist, as if the two had ever been separable for him, or for anyone.

Late in his life, a reporter asked Baldwin if he still had hope. He didn't answer right away. Then he said, "Hope is invented every day." Not found. Not inherited. Invented. Built. Carried forward. Even when it resisted being carried. That daily act of invention took its toll, and Baldwin was tired. The later essays are sharper, angrier, more direct, and less willing to compromise. He wrote like a man who had given the best of himself to a country that never quite knew what to do with him. He called out Reagan-era lies. He refused to obscure the cost of American innocence. He said aloud what no one else dared, and the more fiercely he told the truth, the more solitary he became.

That's the thing about clarity. It isolates.

People say they want honesty, but not when it points at them. Baldwin named what most people spend their lives dodging, and when that truth got too close, too sharp, too clear, people backed away. His clarity put him at odds with other activists as well. He believed in resistance, but not in purity. He saw through systems, but also through people. He wasn't always aligned with Black nationalist movements or younger radicals who demanded sharper ideological lines. Some called him too soft. Others, too strident. He rejected performative anger, yet never denied it was earned.

He'd always been difficult to place. Too Black for white liberals. Too queer for the Black church. Too American for Paris, and too French for Harlem. Too political for the literary elite, yet too literary for the political elite. Baldwin crossed every border and ended up belonging to none of them. That was his strength as much as the reason for his isolation.

Baldwin exposed the machinery behind injustice. The ways it was rationalized and disguised. He wanted to show how the system worked, what it meant to be trapped inside a story someone else wrote for you, and what it took to start rewriting it from the inside. That's also what made his later years lonelier. His writing no longer matched the appetite of the moment. Audiences wanted easy heroes. Baldwin was never that. He was something riskier. He held up the truth and made people see themselves. By the end of his life, most had stopped looking.

In his final years, even his old publisher hesitated to release his final works. Friends had been urging him for years to write something shorter and more contained, another *Notes of a Native Son*, but for a long time the world still showed up when he spoke. That changed near the end. The interviews dried up. The big profile pieces that had once framed him as the conscience of a generation disappeared. He was still writing, still showing up, still speaking, but the rooms kept shrinking. Still, Baldwin didn't stop. Even when the world turned away, he offered it the truth because it was necessary. That's why those late books matter. He didn't care if the room was empty. He wrote what had to be said.

Baldwin once said, "You think your pain and your heartbreak are unprecedented in the history of the world, but then you read." That's what his work offered: recognition and witness. He wanted people to feel seen, even if it hurt. Especially if it hurt. Baldwin gave the facts, even when they stung. It's what kept his work alive long after the applause faded. He wrote because something was at stake. In *The Fire Next Time*, he addressed his nephew directly. In *Giovanni's Room*, he told the story of a man split open by desire and shame. In *No Name in the Street*, he captured betrayal, not only by the country that promised freedom but also by the movements that claimed to fight for it. Baldwin never claimed to have answers, offered no neat solutions. What he gave was writing from inside the wound, raw and unresolved. Some readers followed him there, but most turned away.

There's a reason Baldwin's essays are taught more often than his later books, and a reason the most anthologized quotes are the ones that lean toward hope. Baldwin tore up the ground to reveal what was buried underneath. He was willing to say the things no one wanted to hear: that love without justice is only sentiment, that power rarely listens until it's forced to, that white innocence is a fantasy built on Black suffering, that to live as a queer Black man in America was to live in a body the country would rather erase. He said all of it without flinching and without denying the weight. Baldwin believed in earned clarity, not easy truth, and he knew its cost. Still, he showed up. He wrote and he risked being hated for it.

That's a vital story we're not telling nearly enough.

We live in a time when clarity is often mistaken for cruelty. Comfort is valued more than honesty. Baldwin never softened the blow. He just told it straight. He reminds us that speaking plainly about injustice isn't mean; it's moral. If it isolates you, so be it. When Baldwin left America, he wanted to see the truth without anyone shouting over him. Paris didn't heal him, but it let him keep his eyes open. He called himself a witness, not a judge. For him, that was a moral line, not an emotional one. A judge hands down sentences. A witness testifies, and the world has to live with it.

He saw the same American dynamics replicated in colonial structures. He saw how whiteness operated across borders, how empire dressed itself up in civility and then blamed the brokenness on the people it exploited. From Istanbul to Paris to London to Harlem, the pattern repeated: power made the mess and then blamed anyone too poor or too strange to get out of it. Reviews turned hostile. The money dried up. Movements shifted without him. Still, he wrote.

His later work, like *Just Above My Head*, was longer and less polished. Critics said it meandered. Some called it angry, others said it lacked focus, but the people who read it closely knew better. They saw the same fire, the same ache, the same demand for truth. He wrote like it mattered more to be honest than to be liked. He wrote like someone still trying to reach people, still trying to say: Look. Look at what we've done to each other. Look at what we could become if we stopped pretending we've already made it.

Quoting Baldwin is simple. Living up to what he demanded is something else entirely. It's easier to assign him in a syllabus than to reckon with how much of what he warned us about is still happening. It's not just the politics. It's the posture, the defensiveness, and the insistence that any critique must be framed in the gentlest possible terms or else it doesn't count. Baldwin refused to frame things gently because the people he was writing about didn't get treated gently. They got jail cells and backhands and slurs and silence. They got laws that pretended to be neutral and churches that pretended to love them. Baldwin didn't think the job of the writer was to comfort the powerful. He thought it was to say what needs to be said and then deal with the consequences. So he did.

He never stopped loving his country, but it rarely loved him back in the ways that mattered. It demanded his brilliance, his articulation, his moral vision, and then resented him for the mirror he held up. He kept showing up anyway, but being the one who names the truth comes at a cost, especially when the truth is painful and the audience isn't ready. Baldwin was embraced when his critiques could be framed as literary, dismissed when they became too direct. He said the problem wasn't just history, it was now. He pointed out that white Americans didn't want to be freed from racism because they still enjoyed its benefits. He knew that once the truth began to sting, people stopped listening.

There's a long tradition of demanding emotional labor from the marginalized, asking them to educate, to explain, to forgive in real time. Baldwin did more than his share of that, but what makes his work endure is his precision. He described what was broken and then made you feel it, and he made it impossible to pretend that any of this could be fixed with kindness alone. The world still rewards the story that hurts the least, not the one that lands closest to the truth. Being clear cost him nearly everything. That's also why we're still reading him. Clarity isn't safe, but it lasts.

Baldwin knew clarity could cost you the room. He told the truth anyway and kept telling it after the room began to empty. What survives in his work is the force of a man who refused to distort truth just to make it easier for the world to hear.

Francisco Goya

Francisco Goya painted monsters onto the walls of his house. These were monsters, real as nightmares, painted in private on the plaster of his home. A god eating his child. A dog lost in a sea of nothing. Witches hunched in shadow. Old men crumbling at the edges. A landscape stripped of light. He gave them no titles, offered no explanations, and never showed them to anyone. They were discovered only after his death, seeping from the walls of the Quinta del Sordo, the House of the Deaf Man.

Imagine that room and the plaster whispering horrors. Goya saw too much. He lived through revolutions, executions, invasions, betrayals. This was the bloodiest stretch of Spain's history, and he didn't look away. He painted because someone had to document what was happening. Like Baldwin, he understood that seeing clearly leaves you with a single obligation: to witness, even if no one else wants to know. *The Black Paintings*, originally painted on the plaster around him, are a vision without disguise, a final effort to make sense of a world determined not to.

For most of his early career, Goya was exactly what the system wanted him to be: charming, prolific, and fashionable. He painted elegant portraits, designed tapestries for the royal court, and rose steadily through the ranks of official favor. Goya had talent and timing. Spain wanted to appear stable and cultured, and Goya knew how to deliver that. Still, under the surface, there was always a restlessness and a reluctance to paint a world he knew was a lie.

His early portraits, even when flattering, carried an undercurrent of tension. His etchings poked at hypocrisy and ignorance. He had a way of seeing past appearances, of catching people in the moment just after the mask slipped off.

Then, in 1793, he got sick. No one knows exactly what it was, maybe syphilis or lead poisoning, maybe something else entirely, but it changed him. He survived, but his hearing never came back. He was thirty-seven, newly deaf, and abruptly separated from the world he'd once moved through so easily. From that point on, everything in his art got sharper, angrier, and, above all, more honest. He'd always been perceptive, but now he was utterly relentless. He started drawing the things most people preferred to forget: torture, famine, corruption, even madness. Not the suffering that inspires sympathy, but the kind that leaves scars and refuses comfort. He had been a court painter, and now he was something more dangerous. A man with nothing left to prove and everything left to say.

The Peninsular War shattered any remaining illusions. Napoleon's forces invaded Spain in 1808, and what followed was a nightmare. Guerrilla fighters were executed in public squares. Civilians were mutilated, raped, and massacred. The French claimed they were bringing enlightenment, but all they seemed to bring was horror and death. Goya saw all of it. He saw what it did to people, how it warped them, how it stripped away pretense until only terror, vengeance, and ruin remained. While others tried to shape a heroic narrative, Goya picked up his brush and told the truth.

The Second of May 1808 and *The Third of May 1808* are among the most famous paintings of the war. In *The Third of May 1808*, a man stands before a firing squad, arms raised, terror written across his features. The soldiers are faceless; their rifles form a wall. The ground is streaked with blood, and there is no heroism in this moment before death. The light shows everything. When *The Third of May 1808* was finally displayed publicly, decades after Goya's death, critics argued over whether it was too raw, too emotional, too political. That wasn't how art was supposed to work. History paintings were meant to ennoble, to flatter, to freeze sacrifice into something that could be admired. Goya gave them something else entirely: grief instead of glory, terror instead of triumph, the moment just before death, and the certainty that it would keep happening. He painted war as infection, a disease that seeps into a country's bones and makes cruelty feel ordinary. Absorbing his work is difficult because he doesn't offer relief, but even these paintings don't fully capture what he documented.

His series of etchings, *The Disasters of War*, is where the real indictment lives. It's eighty-two images with no names, no glory, just mangled bodies, twisted faces, piles of the dead and the dying. Victims and perpetrators were both rendered with the same unsparing eye. There are no heroes and no clean lines between good and evil, only suffering. Goya doesn't frame the violence with allegory or distance; he shows mutilated corpses, women being assaulted, bodies torn, hung, discarded. The captions are blunt. "This is worse." "One cannot look." "Why?" There is no narrative comfort and no resolution, just the question: how did we let this happen? He painted the bystanders too, the ones who watched, the ones who profited, and the ones who pretended not to see. Goya understood that witnessing isn't neutral, a truth some artists still try to avoid. You either name what is happening, or you become complicit in the silence that lets it continue. That so many of these images still feel contemporary isn't proof of his foresight; it's an indictment of our continued refusal to change.

He didn't publish them in his lifetime. He knew what they were. He called the series *Fatal Consequences of the Bloody War in Spain with Bonaparte*. A mouthful, but accurate. These were receipts, not political cartoons, as I've sometimes seen them described when exhibited now. Goya faced it head-on and made it impossible for others to pretend they hadn't seen. He forced violence into focus and made it impossible to ignore. Goya's horrors were personal, a record of what happens when nobody is willing to face the human cost of conflict.

The war ended, but the nightmare didn't. The Spanish monarchy was restored under King Ferdinand VII, a ruler so repressive he made Napoleon look like a minor inconvenience. Censorship returned along with the Inquisition and torture. Once again, Goya found himself surrounded by the worst kind of silence, the kind that cloaks cruelty in piety. He was nearly seventy, after decades as a court painter and still on the books under a king he despised, but instead of retiring into comfort or compliance, he turned inward and made some of the most haunting images ever put to any surface.

The Black Paintings were brushed directly onto the walls of his home, Quinta del Sordo, the House of the Deaf Man, a fitting name for a house that heard no sound but still absorbed every scream. They weren't meant for public view, so there are no titles on the walls, but we've since given them names like *Saturn Devouring His Son*, *Witches' Sabbath*, *The Fates*. These works sit there, raw and unrelenting. *Saturn Devouring His Son* shows a god ripping into the body of his child with eyes wide and ravenous, as if he can't stop himself (Plate 3). It is myth rendered as trauma and power shown in its most grotesque, primal form.

Remember, this wasn't in a gallery, it was in Goya's dining room. He lived surrounded by them. The house became a kind of mausoleum, not of bodies, but of illusions. When you hold back for too long, the truth seeps out anyway, in this case onto walls and into memory. Goya had no one left to impress, so he painted what remained: fear, madness, and the monstrous hunger of unchecked power. Yet even in the bleakest of *The Black Paintings*, a trace of humanity lingers. A hand reaches out. A figure turns toward another, caught mid-motion, neither recoil nor comfort. Goya didn't paint hope, but he sometimes let it flicker at the edges. It was worn down, unheroic, not enough to save anyone, but still proof that humanity hadn't vanished altogether.

The Black Paintings were never meant for public eyes, and maybe that's why they could tell so much truth, but they didn't stay hidden. Decades after his death they were cut from the walls and moved into the museum light. The ugliness wasn't just about war or power or the church, but about what happens when a whole society looks away. Spain had become a place where silence meant safety and cruelty became routine. Even his portraits reveal the shift. Years before the worst of the repression, the royal family and their circle still sat for him, but whatever reverence he had once offered was already eroding. In *Charles IV of Spain and His Family*, the king and queen are mannequin-stiff, faces heavy, eyes flat. Goya stands off in the background, both participant and outsider, a quiet accusation against the very people who paid him. He survived because no one wanted to see what he had put in plain sight.

Yet, I've taken some license in this retelling, because Goya never fully explained himself. He had lived through the invasion and occupation in Madrid, close enough to see bodies in the streets and to hear stories that never made it into official history, but he rarely said how particular scenes had reached him. Most of the *Disasters of War* etchings remain untitled and undated. He left them unpublished during his lifetime. Whether that choice came from fear, exhaustion, or strategy is still debated. There's no record of him defending their value. Maybe it mattered more that they existed. The images were carved into copper and left to speak for themselves. That silence, too, is part of his legacy. He trusted the images to carry the weight, he let the horror stand without embellishment, and he left it to the viewer to either face it or turn away. Either way, the responsibility was no longer his alone. He'd seen too much to pretty it up, and he knew what the lie looked like. The lie said violence was necessary, that suffering was justified, and that some people just mattered less than others. He'd heard it from both sides: French and Spanish, royals and rebels. No one had clean hands, and Goya didn't pretend otherwise. Instead, he gave us pictures that refuse to be explained away. These are images that stop you cold. Images that ask: if this was the cost, who paid it, and who decided it was worth it?

That's what makes his later work so unbearable and so necessary at the same time. Goya showed us what we were capable of ignoring. He saw violence wrapped in the language of honor and cruelty excused in the name of order, neutrality claimed by those who simply turned away. He painted because the lie had gotten too loud, and the truth needed form. Two centuries later, the images still land as sharply as they did then because we keep finding new ways to look away, new euphemisms, new disguises. Goya had no use for that kind of abstraction. He gave us limbs, screams, and aftermath. He gave us indisputable evidence of our crimes.

When we flinch at Goya's work today, it's because we recognize these scenes. The outstretched arm, the terrified face, the moment before the end: we see them not only in museums, but in news footage, in headlines, and in every replayed disaster. Now those faces are pixelated and compressed, looping until they lose their sting. Horror is everywhere, but constant exposure dulls its effect. Goya painted to pierce that numbness and to make the violence impossible to ignore because it never really ended. Those images became templates. Goya wanted us to feel the truth long enough that we had no choice but to remember what we'd done.

This is the heart of it: refusing to look away. Art can't stop war, but it can dismantle the stories that make war sound reasonable. Goya painted what people permitted, not just what they endured. He showed horror as contagion, spreading because too many allowed it. As he aged, his portraits darkened, bodies warped, faces twisted, his shadows lengthened. Even his brushwork took on its own violence.

The Disasters of War was necessary because a lie can become so familiar it starts to feel like fact. Goya's work broke that illusion. It said: No. This is what it was. This is what we did. He documented complicity because violence takes more than one form. Sometimes it's loud, with cannons, executions, and war, but other times it's quiet, propelled by bureaucracy, denial, or the decision that what's happening isn't your problem. Goya painted both, and he didn't let the viewer off the hook.

Even now, museums sometimes struggle with how to present his work. *The Black Paintings* resist explanation. The *Disasters of War* series resists display. They're not easy to place next to the landscapes and nudes that fill the rest of the gallery. They accuse and unsettle. That's the point.

Goya didn't live to see most of these works displayed. The *Disasters of War* series wasn't made public until decades after his death. *The Black Paintings* were literally stripped from the walls of his home and moved to a museum without explanation or context. For years, critics treated them like curiosities, unsettling but not central. It took more than a century for the art world to start reckoning with what Goya had actually done: broken the rules of representation so completely that even modern viewers still struggle to absorb it.

The truth he painted got shelved until we could stomach it. Goya was asking us to remember not only the blood and the broken bodies, but the choice to look away. The stories we tell ourselves to make the violence bearable, or to push it off as distant, exceptional, or temporary. But the violence was none of those things, and neither was Goya. He spent his later years in exile, living in France, half-forgotten by the same court that once relied on him. The final portraits are smaller with looser brushwork, the color almost gone. He'd already said what he needed to say. What mattered was whether anyone would listen.

Clarity exacts a cost. Goya didn't flinch from brutality, and he never confused it for heroism. He didn't romanticize suffering; he put it on the wall, unfiltered. Telling the truth that directly isn't just a risk to power; it corrodes the witness too. Goya was already deaf, aging, half-exiled, and still he painted, still he faced truth. The price for refusing to look away was steep. It stripped him of his comfort, distance, and any hope that his honesty would be rewarded, but he kept painting. What we rarely admit is not just that he saw what others refused, but that he never let himself forget. Goya understood that witnessing has its own cost. Even in silence and exile, he made forgetting impossible. Sometimes art's job is to make the truth undeniable.

Artists like Käthe Kollwitz and Otto Dix carried that legacy forward, showing the cost of violence without hiding the details. Kollwitz set grief into stone, Dix painted the aftermath of war in grotesque detail. They weren't simply following Goya; they were answering him, extending the demand: if you've seen it, you don't get to pretend you haven't. There are moments when beauty deceives, when silence becomes complicity, when art's most urgent task is to stop us from pretending we didn't know. We still live in a world where denial comes easily. The pull to look away is strong, but so is the obligation to resist it. Goya made sure the truth endured. Distance is a luxury for the comfortable. For those who can't look away, what remains is honesty, even when it unsettles everyone else.

Mary Shelley

Mary Shelley wrote *Frankenstein* while mourning her dead daughter. That part rarely makes it into the ghost story anthologies. We like to start in the parlor of Villa Diodati, with a stormy night, crackling fire, Byron and Polidori lounging dramatically as Percy quotes Coleridge and Mary dreams up a monster. It's a good story, and it's the one I grew up with, too, but it's only a fraction of what she actually lived.

The baby had died months earlier. Her name was Clara. The loss never left her, not even in dreams. Mary kept dreaming that Clara came back to life. "I dream that my little baby came to life again," she wrote in her journal that March. "That it had only been cold, and that we rubbed it by the fire, and it lived." But Clara didn't come back. Mary was eighteen, exiled from her family, and haunted by the suicides of her half-sister Fanny Godwin and Percy's first wife Harriet Westbrook in the wake of their elopement. She grieved in silence while Percy found comfort elsewhere. She was just trying to make it through the night. "I busied myself to think of a story," she recalled later, "one which would speak to the mysterious fears of our nature and awaken thrilling horror." What she wrote came from grief, stitched together and brought to life, far from the horror stories people expected.

Frankenstein emerged as a reckoning. It asked what happens when we bring something into the world and then abandon it. What happens when you create something, life, art, a future, or anything and it won't stop suffering? Mary already knew that question by heart. She just gave it flesh. Shelley was living in the shadow of other ghosts too. Her mother, Mary Wollstonecraft, had died giving birth to her. Her father, William Godwin, had raised her on radical ideals and then disowned her when she ran off with Percy Shelley. Her half-sister Fanny was left behind when Mary and Percy fled to France with Mary's stepsister Claire Clairmont; two years later Fanny killed herself with laudanum. Not long after, Percy's pregnant wife drowned herself in a lake. Mary had grown up in a world where words were supposed to change things. Her parents believed that and passed that belief on to her, but by the time she was nineteen, the world had already shown her what ideas were worth to a body in pain.

Shelley wrote from experience, from knowing what it means to be haunted by loss, by failure, by the parts of love that never save you, and by creations you can't undo. The creature in the novel isn't a villain, but a question that won't resolve. He's grief given form, stitched from the wrongs no one wanted to face. When he begs his creator for care, for connection, for meaning, he's asking the same thing Mary was asking of the world. Why did you bring me into this if you weren't going to stay? She wrote sorrow, not just science fiction. Her monster was never just about the surface reading of science gone awry, but about grief left unspoken, and the loneliness of being created and abandoned.

She knew what that felt like. Percy believed in freedom, but mostly for himself. When their son William died, Mary collapsed. Percy kept writing about liberty, slept with her friends, and called her sorrow inconvenient. She turned to the only thing that hadn't betrayed her—writing. When the creature says, "I am alone and miserable," it's confession. When he begs, "I ought to be thy Adam, but I am rather the fallen angel," he's not just talking to Victor. He's talking to anyone who's ever reached for love and found only empty hands.

She was inventing a container for everything that had nowhere else to go. Her dead mother. Her dead child. The way Percy looked at her like a muse and then left her to carry the weight. The way her circle kept mistaking cruelty or carelessness for genius. *Frankenstein* was a reckoning, and it worked, not because it was flawless; it wasn't, but because it faced the truth. The monster is stitched together from scraps. Mary was, too. Everyone who keeps going after loss is. So is the novel itself. She pulled from everything: theology, philosophy, nightmares, revolution, the ache of watching someone you love vanish. The whole book reads like it's trying to stitch the world back together and doesn't quite succeed, but it doesn't have to because what Mary Shelley did was brave. She wrote through devastation instead of around it. She didn't hide pain behind symbols; she made it loud. The monster is desperate, the story always nearer to collapse than closure. That's why it endures. It never pretends there's no wound.

Shelley never knew her mother. Mary Wollstonecraft died eleven days after giving birth. The absence didn't keep her daughter from feeling her presence. Her mother's legend hung over her like a challenge she could never escape. Mary Shelley grew up with her mother's actual words. People read her books, repeated her words, and visited her tomb as if it were a shrine. What do you do when your origin story begins in grief and ends in genius? You try to live up to it. Mary tried. Her life didn't follow a clean arc. She didn't become her mother. She became a runaway, a widow, and a writer. She made a new genre while bleeding from every part of her life. Hers is a story of devastation remade into invention.

Despite what you may have read, Mary didn't just conjure *Frankenstein* in a flash of inspiration at a party. She wrote it at eighteen, while grieving her daughter, ostracized by her family, and exiled from polite society. The creature was born from loss, not fantasy. Mary knew what it meant to be abandoned. Three of her four children died before reaching age four: one to dysentery, one to malaria, one to an unnamed illness. She kept their memories in lockets and their dates in her journal.

Frankenstein is the one people remember, but it wasn't her only act of literary defiance. After Percy drowned, his body found with a copy of Keats in his coat and his heart refusing to burn on the funeral pyre (a story that smells of mythmaking, but we'll come back to that), Mary kept going. She wrote novels, biographies, edited Percy's poems to protect his legacy, and supported herself and her surviving son in a world that rewarded neither female independence nor female authorship.

She could live with the contradictions. She loved a man who abandoned his pregnant wife, revered a mother she never met, and built a genre on dread without letting it consume her. That's the part we forget. Mary Shelley wasn't only the first voice of modern horror; she was also a writer who believed in continuation. Her monsters were mirrors and in those mirrors, she saw herself, fragmented but still standing. The world tried to shrink her: first as a scandal, then as a widow, then as a footnote in her husband's mythology but Mary Shelley was never a vessel for someone else's brilliance.

She could have disappeared, as so many women did, widowed, disgraced, and hollowed out by loss. Instead, she reshaped herself. She refused to glamorize pain or drape it in romanticism, choosing instead to write straight from the rawness of every difficult feeling. *The Last Man* is a dystopia that reads like a warning bell for everything she had already endured: a world emptied by plague, marked by absence, haunted by the unsaved. Critics dismissed it as too bleak and too personal. She knew exactly what she was doing.

She outlived them all, every critic, every skeptic, not just in years, but in work, in resilience, in the refusal to stop writing when no one was asking for her ideas. She wrote novels, biographies, travel essays, and political commentary. Most of it has been forgotten, but none of it was careless. She was always trying to build a frame around chaos, to give shape to the unshapable. She never claimed devastation had a moral, only refused to let it be the end of her story. In *Lodore* and *Falkner*, she gave us women negotiating ruin, not escaping it, haunted yet still shaping something new from the debris. These are characters with no illusions left who kept choosing life anyway.

I said we'd come back to it so, let's talk about how she literally kept Percy's heart. As the story goes, it wouldn't burn on his funeral pyre, so a friend pulled it from the ashes and gave it to her. She wrapped it in his last poem and kept it in her desk drawer. People call it a darkly romantic gesture. If it really happened, I'd be more inclined to call it unending grief. She carried that grief with her through every loss that followed. She carried the memory of children who didn't survive, debts that never stopped piling up, and a publishing world that dismissed her as a teenager who got lucky instead of the writer who had created a book with staying power. Mary believed, as perhaps we all should, that meaning came from what you did next. She kept her eyes forward, not back.

She lived through burial after burial, betrayal after betrayal, and still, she found her way back to the page. She was brilliant, but most people miss that she was resilient in a way that never stopped costing her. She wrote through grief to understand it. *Frankenstein* was the beginning of a life spent asking: What can be made from ruin? What still deserves to be said when everything else is gone? She kept answering that question, again and again, with her writing.

After Percy's death, the literary world mostly tried to forget her. They published him, quoted him, canonized him. Mary was treated as a footnote, called widow, editor, muse, but never recognized as the mind behind one of the most enduring novels in English literature and never as the writer who kept working even while the world stripped her bare.

She moved back to England with her son and rebuilt her life from almost nothing. There was no money, no status, and no protection, all hard to imagine now as the fate of Percy Shelley's widow, a literary icon herself whose stature would later eclipse his own in some circles. There were only the stories she wasn't finished telling, and she told them. Quietly, furiously, and beautifully. She kept writing, not as much and not as visibly, but she didn't stop. In the years after Percy's death, she produced *Valperga*, *Perkin Warbeck*, *Lodore*, and *Falkner*, books that were both survival and expression. She was a single mother who needed income, but she also needed form, some way to contain a grief that shifted shape but never really left her. These later novels never drew the attention of *Frankenstein*, but they circled the same haunted questions about power, creation, and the stories we invent to survive ourselves.

The Last Man was something different. I might even love it more than *Frankenstein*.

Published in 1826, it wasn't meant to charm or console. It was prophetic: a ruined future emptied by plague, less about the end of the world than the loneliness of surviving it. Mary poured her mourning into those pages. Lionel, the narrator, wanders the ruins alone after everyone he loves is gone. Critics dismissed it as too much, too bleak, too raw. They missed that she was making grief mythic, naming the price of outliving everyone you love.

She had buried Percy. She had buried three of her four children. She was only twenty-eight. *The Last Man* offers persistence, and the ache of living past the point where life still makes sense. It's not a novel about apocalypse but about aftermath, about the world's insistence on continuing even after meaning has drained away, and about writing as the last tether to something real.

Mary Shelley lived with devastation but never let it swallow her whole. She shaped meaning from loss with her pen, her words, and her refusal to disappear. Resilience for her was quiet, the kind that turned grief into art and let her outlast her era. The muted spaces in her work, the restraint, are signs of strength rather than surrender. She made the tragedy of her world into narratives that both acknowledged and transcended the limits of what could be known and shared. Her legacy is the monster, but it's also the quiet work, the places where she uncovered truths beneath catastrophe. In those spaces, she showed that survival is sometimes about what you refuse to let go of, and that the real power lies in shaping something from the wreckage.

Frankenstein was a warning about the force of grief and the human capacity to rebuild, even when what we create in the aftermath carries the scars of its origins. Shelley's work helped teach me that devastation doesn't have to be the end. It can be the beginning of something more profound, something that emerges only when we're willing to face the darkness directly.

That's why this chapter ends not with *Frankenstein* but with *The Last Man*. *Frankenstein* was the gift she gave the world. *The Last Man* was the one she kept for herself: a quieter, lonelier book, dismissed and ignored, set aside on the shelf. In many ways, it's the more honest novel. Its subject is loss, the shape grief leaves behind, the questions it never resolves, and the way it hollows out an imagined future. She wrote because some truths have to be shaped into language before they stop swallowing you whole.

If you've ever tried to make sense of the unthinkable, Mary Shelley left a record of what it looks like. She wrote her way through devastation, carving meaning by staring straight at what hurt. Her work doesn't offer comfort so much as instruction: keep writing, keep building, even when the ground feels scorched. In the worst moments, the work may be the only next step. Even in loss, it's possible to move forward and shape what's to come.

In the end, Mary Shelley offered a model of endurance that isn't about bouncing back as if it never happened but about taking the next step with the damage still there. She showed that devastation changes the work, but doesn't have to end it. Her career reminds us that meaning sometimes has to be built from ruins.

She never argued that suffering makes us noble. By the time Shelley wrote *The Last Man*, she knew too much about what it meant to outlive the world she thought she was building: a marriage, a family, and a shared literary future. She kept writing anyway, long enough to give grief a shape that could endure.

Survival as Art

Some seasons aren't just about brilliance. They're about refusing to disappear.

DMITRI SHOSTAKOVICH | YAYOI KUSAMA | FRANK AUERBACH | SERGEI RACHMANINOFF

Dmitri Shostakovich

Shostakovich opened the morning paper knowing that his life was about to change. A friend had warned him the night before; voice lowered on the phone line everyone knew was tapped: "Tomorrow's *Pravda*. Brace yourself." Still, nothing prepared him for how brutal it felt to see it in black and white. He unfolded the pages, newsprint trembling in his hands, his name thinly veiled in the headline that read "Muddle Instead of Music."

He had always known this moment might come. Success in Stalin's Russia was always a tightrope, and Shostakovich had been walking it for years. His opera, *Lady Macbeth of Mtsensk*, had felt different. It was bold, expressive, and, he thought, a real breakthrough. It thrilled audiences, and critics praised it lavishly. For a brief moment, he let himself hope for real artistic freedom. Now he felt foolish for believing it. The *Pravda* review, Stalin's own mouthpiece, tore into the opera without mercy, calling it chaotic, dissonant, and dangerously formalist. Each sentence was a death knell, not just for his career, but maybe for his life.

The article accused him of mocking the Russian people, betraying socialist ideals, and worst of all, of losing touch with "the healthy tastes of the Soviet masses." That was Stalin's shorthand: fall back in line or vanish. As he read, his throat tightened. A familiar nausea twisted deep inside. He scanned each brutal sentence twice, hoping irrationally to find some hidden relief, some loophole that might offer him cover. There was none.

He folded the paper, set it on the table, and stared into the empty room. This was a verdict. Artists had been disappeared for far less. For a moment, he imagined fleeing, giving up music, trying to live quietly somewhere beyond reach. The thought passed almost as quickly as it came. He knew he would never stop.

He reached for his notebook, flipped to a fresh page, pencil hovering. Silence was safer, but silence meant letting them win. He knew how dangerous his next notes could be, but some things still needed to be said, carefully, quietly, but unmistakably. He steadied his hand, drew a breath, and began.

The pencil scratched against paper, filling the quiet with a familiar comfort. Shostakovich composed carefully, each note chosen like a secret message he hoped someone, someday, might decode. He remembered the advice whispered among fellow artists: "Make your meaning clear enough to matter but hidden enough to survive." It was the only way to endure under Stalin, a leader who took the arts personally, punishing any hint of subversion swiftly and permanently.

That morning, as he sketched out themes for what would become his *Fifth Symphony*, Shostakovich knew survival meant subtlety. The Party had just turned on his opera *Lady Macbeth of Mtsensk*, denouncing its brutal sex, corrupt officials, and blaring, chaotic climaxes as vulgar, formalist, and anti-Soviet. Stalin had heard mockery in the shrieks and crashes, not loyalty. Whatever was left of his outrage now had to be disguised. So he began cautiously, notes precise and understated, disguising lament as reverence and criticism as loyalty. Each bar was an exercise in restraint, each crescendo a careful calculation: How much could he say without drawing fire?

He stopped when footsteps passed in the hallway outside his apartment, his heart quickening until the sound faded. Paranoia followed him everywhere, but it was more than just that. By then, his opera had already been denounced in *Pravda*, colleagues had vanished into prisons and work camps, and everyone in Moscow knew what unexpected footsteps at night could mean. It was a survival skill. He had learned to expect sudden knocks at the door, polite questions with dangerous edges, invitations he dared not refuse. Fear had become part of his daily practice, another instrument he knew how to play.

At the desk, he returned to his work, the memory of Stalin at the theater rising again. A year had passed since that night and the *Pravda* denunciation that followed, but he still saw the dictator grimacing, whispering to his aides, then leaving before the opera had finished. That gesture had been a sentence in itself. In the stillness of his apartment, Shostakovich understood how far he had already gone. The next step would have to be taken with great care.

The *Fifth Symphony* began to take shape. Outwardly, it spoke the language of Soviet triumph, but within it carried mourning for the freedoms already lost. Its meaning lay in shadows, audible only to those willing to listen closely. He paused often, measuring the danger. To compose honestly was to live perpetually on edge, balanced between expression and betrayal. Yet the music pressed forward, insistent, impossible to silence. He'd learned how to bury truths deep in sound, to let every piece serve as a hidden memoir of life under suffocation.

When the symphony premiered months later, the audience rose to its feet. Applause filled the hall, and some listeners wept openly. They heard the long, grieving Largo as a kind of public funeral, a place to mourn friends and neighbors who had simply vanished. They heard the finale's blazing march not as honest joy but as something strained and desperate, triumph shouted until it sounded like a threat. Critics labeled it a return to socialist realism, but those who listened carefully recognized that it was really survival disguised as compliance. That night, back at home, Shostakovich trembled with exhaustion and relief. Against the odds, he had spoken what needed saying, softly enough to escape punishment, but strongly enough to be heard.

His relief didn't last. Dread crept back in with the days that followed. The same voices that praised him could turn against him without warning. Rumors spread that Stalin himself might attend a performance. Would he hear the defiance buried in the score? Would those hidden notes betray their author? Shostakovich walked through sleepless nights with those questions, weighing every possible consequence. Each morning he sat back down, opened his notebook, and began again. His music was written in a kind of code. On the surface, it used the bright, confident language the Party expected, but underneath it carried grief, unease, and private anger. Silence would have been safer, but silence meant surrender.

Shostakovich had begun to understand that in Stalin's Russia, truth was not declared aloud. It was hidden in plain sight, tucked into phrases and motifs, and smuggled quietly into the world with the hope that someone in the future might recognize it. Music became his way of sending messages forward in time. His survival depended less on dazzling invention than on his ability to stay subtle. A symphony could speak in two registers at once: one official and loyal, the other coded and restless. He learned to live that double life, presenting the obedient surface while guarding the more complicated truths within.

The cost was visible. Friends noticed the shadows under his eyes, the way he startled at knocks on the door, and the way he drifted into long, heavy silences in the middle of a conversation. They worried, knowing what happened to artists who slipped. Still, he kept working, revising cautiously, listening for the line he must not cross.

Then came the siege. When German forces encircled Leningrad, Shostakovich was trapped inside. Food disappeared, heat failed, and bodies filled the streets. He queued for the same thin rations as everyone else and joined the conservatory's volunteer fire brigade, climbing up to the roof in a helmet and heavy gloves to watch for incendiary bombs. Officials photographed him there and spread the image across the country, turning him into a smiling symbol of resistance while he lived with the same cold and hunger as his neighbors. When the bombardment grew worse, he finally left with his family in an evacuation east, carrying the unfinished score with him as the one thing he refused to abandon. By candlelight or in the brief hours of daylight, he filled scraps of paper while shells shook the city. Out of that ruin came the first sketches of his *Seventh Symphony*, the "Leningrad." It became a banner of resistance, but beneath its heroic surface ran quieter currents: grief, endurance, and the knowledge that triumph never erased loss. Even in this most patriotic of works, he left reminders that suffering couldn't be cured by patriotism or even victory.

In safety, he completed the score, still aware that officials would inspect every measure for loyalty. At its premiere, the audience wept. Their applause was overwhelming. The state called it a weapon, broadcasting it toward German lines as proof of Soviet resilience. Stalin heard the propaganda he was supposed to hear. Shostakovich hoped others would hear the mourning that lay beneath. For him, the symphony was as much an elegy as a victory cry, a testimony for the countless dead who would otherwise vanish from record.

Praise from above felt like another form of control. Success narrowed his options instead of expanding them, binding him more tightly to the demands of the state. Under that pressure, he turned to chamber works, quartets, and smaller forms that seemed too private to attract official attention. There he could speak more plainly. The quartets were stripped of grandeur, intimate and direct, filled with sorrow, longing, and fragile hope. To a friend, he confided, "My quartets are my letters in bottles, thrown into a vast, dangerous sea." It was the truest description of what he was doing. He was sending his voice out where it might someday be heard. Until then, he kept writing, every note balanced against the risk of being noticed.

Years passed, and Stalin's shadow remained over every page Shostakovich wrote. He never lost the habit of glancing over his shoulder or pausing at sudden sounds in the hallway. Survival had become second nature. Then, one evening in 1953, came the news that Stalin was dead. Shostakovich felt disbelief rather than relief. The man who had ruled his life through fear was gone, yet his absence brought not freedom but uncertainty. Slowly, the air shifted. Shostakovich spoke a little more openly, not with abandon, but with measured candor. In letters and interviews, he allowed himself small flashes of honesty about what he had lived through under Stalin: the public denunciations, the nights waiting for a knock at the door, the siege of Leningrad, the friends who never came back. He stayed cautious, but he refused to pretend the terror hadn't happened or that the dead could be waved away.

In his later works, he became more direct. The music turned inward, stripped of disguises, more like confession than code. Tension still lingered, but the weight of consequence had eased enough for him to speak more plainly. Looking back near the end, he wrote, "I said what I could say, as clearly as I could afford to say it." That clarity, earned and deliberate, was its own kind of courage. He had whispered, and he had kept whispering long enough that the truth couldn't stay buried forever.

After Stalin's death, the state restored him to favor. He was praised, decorated, and even held up as a cultural hero. Shostakovich wore those honors uneasily. He knew they could disappear as quickly as they'd come. Too often he'd seen friends gone overnight, reputations erased, freedoms stripped away.

He carried the memory of the silenced. He spoke their names in private, as if in prayer, knowing that his own survival owed as much to chance as to caution. He never forgot how fragile it was. That knowledge pressed itself into his final quartets, especially the Fifteenth: stark, pared down, and unguarded. The music trembles near silence, its sparse notes like confessions spoken after years of restraint. By then, he seemed ready to be heard without concealment, whatever the cost. These late works gave listeners a rare view of his grief, a reckoning with decades of guarded speech. He sometimes worried aloud that no one truly grasped the price he'd paid to keep composing. Yet audiences recognized it. They heard, in the taut quiet of his music, echoes of their own lives lived under watch.

He kept composing until illness made it impossible. Even then he wondered if he had said enough. When he died, thousands of artists, colleagues, and even ordinary citizens came to his funeral. They mourned the survivor as much as the composer, remembering the way his music had kept them company in silence. Every note had been a reminder that endurance itself could be resistance. His work still carries that lesson. The truth is always dangerous, Shostakovich teaches. Say it with care if you must but do say it.

In the years after Shostakovich's death, critics and listeners continued to argue over what his music really meant. Some dismissed him as a product of Soviet pressure, a composer who bent too often just to survive. Others cast him as a hidden dissident whose every bar was rebellion in disguise. Neither portrait fully captured him. His truth lived in ambiguity, in layers of meaning that resisted simple explanation. His legacy was in the gray spaces he cultivated so carefully. To listen closely is to hear his scores as maps of a constrained yet determined life, cautious on the surface but fiercely alive underneath. Each symphony became an argument with power. Sit with a quartet and it reads like a journal, fragments of his private world left open to those who could hear. His work documented the human cost of living under a system that demanded silence.

Decades later, his music still feels urgent. New generations hear in it not just secrets of a vanished regime, but an invitation to think about their own silences and compromises. Shostakovich reminds us that courage doesn't have to shout. Rebellion doesn't always declare itself. Sometimes bravery lives in the choice to keep speaking at all, even if only in whispers.

Today, in his last apartment in Moscow, preserved as a small museum, visitors step into the study where he once worked. They lean over the small grand piano, study the manuscripts under glass, and imagine his pencil moving with careful hesitation. They feel the tension in those notes, the pressure of honesty balanced against survival. Some whisper their own truths there, moved by the example of a man who showed that even guarded honesty still matters.

For anyone who has measured words before speaking, who has swallowed what needed saying, who has whispered when shouting was impossible, Shostakovich offers permission. Speak, even if you must do it carefully. Speak, even if you can only do it through ambiguity. Soft voices last. They echo long after the louder ones fade.

When orchestras perform his works today, the same tension between obedience and expression hovers over the music. Conductors linger over the scores, debating phrasing, weighing how much to reveal. Listeners close their eyes and hear questions left without answers. The questions are as alive now as they were then.

Shostakovich knew he would be misunderstood. He expected the charge of cowardice, especially from people looking back from safer times who would see only his compromises. They would point to his Party card, his official posts, the patriotic showpieces, even the public statements issued in his name against dissidents, and ask why he had not refused. The alternative inside Stalin's world was reckless honesty, and that would've ended his voice altogether. He chose a different courage, the kind that persists under pressure, the kind that keeps speaking even when forced into whispers. Historians still debate whether he compromised too much. Musicians who live inside his music rarely doubt him. They feel the quiet defiance of a man who refused silence, who carved out space within oppression to keep hold of what mattered most: his voice, steady even when coded.

Near the end of his life, Shostakovich admitted to friends that he wished he could have written without constant watchfulness. He wondered what it would have been like to compose without fear, without hidden meanings. Yet he also recognized the paradox. His music had gained its force because of the pressure that shaped it. Each guarded choice was an answer to necessity. Without those constraints, the depth we now hear in his work might never have emerged. His caution became the crucible that gave him clarity.

Today, anyone who pauses before speaking in a meeting, or hesitates before sending a risky message, feels a small echo of what he lived daily. To choose words carefully, to shape truth so it can be heard without punishment, is an art Shostakovich mastered. Most people eventually face a version of that calculation. He reminds us that it is not weakness. It can be its own form of courage.

His *Fifth Symphony* still fills concert halls and still brings audiences to their feet. Modern listeners, though, hear it differently from those who first encountered it. They recognize not only a score designed to survive censors, but also a declaration that honesty, even disguised, can endure. One critic observed, "Shostakovich spoke through silences as powerfully as through sound, saying carefully what could not be shouted." Students who study his life learn more than harmony and form. They study the discipline of speaking under threat. They search his writings for the voice beneath the camouflage, tracing the ways he chose expression over surrender.

Those who draw closest to him often feel prompted not just to admire, but to imitate. They resolve to speak when silence would be easier, to choose honesty when avoidance promises comfort. His legacy becomes a lesson that applies well beyond music: courage is not measured in volume, nor truth only in bluntness. Persistence, restraint, and carefully chosen words matter, sometimes more than defiance openly declared.

In an age filled with noise and performed certainty, Shostakovich's music itself is the reminder that some truths have to move quietly. His symphonies speak in two voices at once, bright public triumph for the people in power and quieter lines of grief and doubt for anyone listening beneath the surface. His strength wasn't only in creating under pressure, but in insisting on speaking at all. Each performance of his music carries that defiance forward. Every note is an invitation to speak carefully if you must, measure your words if you need to, but do not be silent.

Late in life, Shostakovich remarked, "I don't write music to speak clearly. I write it to make speaking clearly possible." His work carved out a space where honesty could survive. Guarded speech was resistance.

Shostakovich understood the truths people swallow when speaking becomes dangerous. He knew what it meant to measure every disclosure against its cost. Silence may look like safety, but it can just as easily become surrender. In that kind of world, even a carefully weighted truth is an act of resolve.

The world rarely rewards quiet honesty. Yet anyone who's lived under restraint knows both the cost of clarity and the cost of losing it. Shostakovich shows that caution can be strength. It's the discipline to say what you can without letting the risk suppress your meaning entirely. Measured truths matter because they come at a price.

Say them carefully, he teaches.

But do say them.

Yayoi Kusama

She stood outside the gallery window, staring at her own idea on someone else's wall. Polka dots, hers, unmistakably hers, painted across a canvas signed by a man who had recently visited her studio. He'd admired her work, and he'd asked her questions. Now here it was, reframed under his name, hanging in someone else's show, drawing the same luminaries who wouldn't return her calls. Yayoi Kusama had come to New York to be part of the art world, but the art world shut her out.

She didn't make a scene. She rarely did. She simply watched, quiet and alert, her signature black bob perfectly combed, her outfit striking and intentional, half armor, half announcement. She'd shown up again. That's what mattered: she just stood there, visible, undeniable. If they wouldn't let her in, she'd haunt the sidewalk. She would spend decades like this, at the edge of recognition, always present, never quite allowed. The Japanese woman in a white, male world. People called her obsessive, unstable, impossible to satisfy. She produced more than anyone wanted and wanted more than anyone would allow. They took from her without including her, but she refused to vanish.

The polka dots came first. Long before the art world. Long before New York. Even before she had language for what was happening inside her head. As a child in Matsumoto, Kusama saw them everywhere, covering the walls, crawling over her hands, expanding across her mother's face like an infection only she could see. The hallucinations came without warning, relentless and terrifying. She heard flowers speaking. Patterns shifted when no one touched them. Reality itself began to slip. One afternoon, she screamed in the middle of class because the ceiling had vanished, replaced, she said, by a swirling sky of dots that pulsed like eyes. Her classmates stared. Her teacher called her unwell. That night, she stayed up sketching what she'd seen, filling the margins of old newspapers, as if recording it might keep it from returning.

Her mother didn't believe her, or maybe she did but chose violence anyway. Kusama was beaten for drawing, for speaking out of turn, and for wanting anything her family hadn't chosen for her. Her father was gone often, and when he was home, he was cruel or unfaithful or both. She was sent to spy on him with other women, punished for what she witnessed, for what she couldn't unsee. Her world was chaos, so she made order. Repetition became safety. Infinity nets, the intricate, endless loops she painted for hours at a time, became the only thing that made the spinning stop.

It was survival long before she thought of it as art.

She feared her mind might one day consume her completely. The visions were involuntary, overwhelming, and sometimes violent. Pumpkins swelled until they filled entire rooms. A single flower multiplied endlessly, blotting out the floor. Some mornings, she woke unable to tell what was real. Art was an attempt at restraint. She drew nets to hold the world in place and painted dots to keep her skin from disappearing.

In postwar Japan, no one talked about mental illness. To be unwell was to be unfit, unmarriageable, and deeply shameful. Even the word "hallucination" carried a social stain. Her family told her to hide it, to get over it, to marry someone who could help conceal the problem. She refused. She drew every day, painted late into the night, and covered surfaces compulsively. When one piece was finished, she started another. Her mother tore up drawings in front of her, but it didn't stop her. The hallucinations didn't go away, but creating gave them form and boundaries, a kind of container for them she could hold in her hands.

By her early twenties, Kusama had begun exhibiting locally, but Japan, in the aftermath of war, had no room for a woman like her. The art establishment was rigid, patriarchal, and nationalistic. Critics dismissed her work as too Western and too strange. One called her paintings "disturbing." She agreed and kept making them, but she knew Japan wouldn't change. If she wanted to be seen, she'd have to leave.

So in 1957, with little money and even less English, she packed her watercolors into a suitcase and boarded a plane to New York. She carried with her a letter of encouragement from Georgia O'Keeffe, a rare kindness after Kusama had written to her out of the blue, asking for advice. O'Keeffe had told her not to give up. That was enough.

In the United States, things were different, but not necessarily better. Psychosis was pathologized, medicated, and often turned into spectacle. Kusama wanted to be seen, not fixed. American artists could be eccentric, even erratic, as long as they were men. Madness in men was mythologized. In women, it was either pitied or dismissed entirely. She couldn't change that, so she made madness her method. Her hallucinations became her aesthetic, and she worked to harness her own instability and translate it into visual space.

Still, New York was brutal. She stepped off the plane with two suitcases and a binder of sketches, completely alone. The city was gray, massive, and much louder than she'd imagined. On her first day, she watched strangers pour into the Whitney Museum and wondered how long it would take for her work to hang on those walls. Years later, it still hadn't. She landed in a scene that barely noticed her except to dismiss her. Galleries were gatekept by white men who didn't know what to do with a Japanese woman who painted obsessively and refused to smile on cue. She lived on rice and scraps, bartered art supplies for rent, and hunted for canvas in dumpsters. At one point, she painted on discarded fabric she pulled from a warehouse floor. Her studio was freezing in winter, sweltering in summer, and still she worked, dot after dot, net after net, piece after piece.

The city was full of noise, steel, ambition, the sound of men declaring what art was and would be. In lofts downtown, white men redefined minimalism, conceptualism, and pop. They name-dropped one another in interviews, traded influence at dinners, and built careers on bold, impersonal statements. Donald Judd stacked metal boxes. Frank Stella insisted, "What you see is what you see." Andy Warhol made irony fashionable, but only when it stayed distant and emotionally flat.

Kusama was none of those things. She was maximalist, personal, messy, and worst of all in that moment, foreign. The same critics who praised repetition in Judd's sculpture called hers "hysterical." The same journalists who described Claes Oldenburg's soft forms as "inventive" shrugged when she covered an entire rowboat in bulbous sewn appendages. According to them, she wasn't being edgy, she was being excessive. That was the difference: she wasn't part of the joke. Even in feminist circles, she was too weird, too solitary, and too far outside the dominant modes of politics or theory. Her race marked her as exotic, her illness made her suspect, and her intensity left her without a place. She was in the room, but no one wanted to stand beside her.

When she began to attract attention, it wasn't the kind she could control. Artists came to see her work and left with her ideas, later masquerading as their own. She watched her concepts reappear in their shows, credited to their names: her soft sculptures, her installations, her use of mirrors, even her relentless repetition. She saw her own vision repackaged and celebrated, but only when presented by men who looked the part. Critics called them innovators. They called her derivative—of them. Sometimes they didn't call her anything at all. One artist had stood in her kitchen staring at a chair she had covered in hand-sewn soft phallic forms, a piece she titled *Accumulation No. 1.* Two months later, he unveiled a couch covered in suggestive and crude fabric tubes. He got a gallery, while she got ignored.

She wasn't invited to the parties, but she showed up anyway. She wore her own art, painted her shoes, and made her presence a kind of performance. She was difficult to overlook, even when they tried. When galleries still refused her, she turned the city into her canvas. She organized "happenings" in Central Park, on Wall Street, at the Venice Biennale. There was public nudity, political protest, and surreal beauty. She painted polka dots on naked bodies and staged anti-war demonstrations where her collaborators held mirrors to the sky. She invited the press, and sometimes they came. Other times, they mocked her. Either way, she kept performing. Her message was clear: if you won't give me a platform, I'll build one. If you won't give me space, I'll take the street.

In 1969, she staged a happening at the Museum of Modern Art, not because they'd invited her, but precisely because they hadn't. She marched in with a band of naked performers painted in dots and conducted what she called the *Grand Orgy to Awaken the Dead.* They danced in the sculpture garden, posing beside bronze and marble works by men who had been canonized while she still fought for a solo show. She read poetry through a megaphone, crowned the nude dancers with flowers, and offered love as protest, absurdity as critique. Security showed up. The press took pictures. The museum didn't acknowledge it, but it happened.

Later, Kusama would call the event a kind of exorcism, a way of forcing her body into a space that refused to acknowledge her. She got tired of waiting. If her work wasn't welcome inside the museum, she'd stage her own show on the lawn. She'd make herself impossible to ignore. It didn't earn her a retrospective, not then, but it made her unforgettable. She was trying to merge with everything, to become so undeniable that no one could pretend not to see her. It was a way to stay visible when everything conspired to push her out.

She built installations of furniture covered in soft phallic forms. She created mirrored rooms that seemed to stretch into infinity, pulling the viewer into the pattern and painted on a scale so vast and repetitive it bordered on the ecstatic. The work exhausted her. It thrilled her. When no one came to buy or collect or canonize, she just kept going.

Eventually, the pressure broke something loose. Her body gave out and her mind soon followed. In the early 1970s, Kusama left New

York and returned to Japan, a country that hadn't wanted her before and still wasn't sure what to do with her now. She was exhausted, broke, and increasingly unwell. The hallucinations never stopped and the anxiety worsened. She began having thoughts of suicide, and then not just thoughts. She needed help so she checked herself into the Seiwa Hospital for the Mentally Ill, a quiet facility in Tokyo, where she chose to remain voluntarily. Most people assumed she'd vanished. She hadn't. She'd simply moved the work to another room.

Her studio near the hospital was barely larger than a closet. The walls were painted white, the windows small and smudged. She lined every surface with paper and began again. Rows of dots, nets, soft sculptures piling like snowdrifts. It was quiet and no one interrupted. She could finally hear herself think. She painted, wrote poems and surreal novels, dense with eroticism and violence, built sculptures, some massive, some delicate, all unmistakably hers. She submitted work to exhibitions and competitions. Sometimes they accepted her. Often they didn't, but she kept sending it. She stayed in the room, even when that room was a ward no one visited and a gallery no one entered. There were years with no calls, no letters, no reviews, and no shows. Just the small studio down the street, blank paper, and the sound of wind moving through hospital curtains. Some days she wondered if she'd been erased entirely, if the city had swallowed her whole and moved on. Even then, she painted.

She painted for hours without speaking. Assistants sometimes found her asleep on the floor, brush still in hand, surrounded by canvases filled edge to edge with nets or dots so small they blurred vision. The studio itself was a rented room near the psychiatric hospital where she lived, paid for with the thin income from her paintings and the strange, visceral novels and poems she began to publish. Her assistants were usually young artists and students who recognized her talent and vision, helping stretch canvases and mix paint on a volunteer basis between their own jobs. She didn't need an audience. She needed rhythm, the act of making, the steady return of pattern to bring her back to herself. "I fight pain, anxiety, and fear every day," she wrote in her journal. "And the only method I have found that relieves my illness is to keep creating art." She never once called the silence a break. She called it her "solitary period," as if solitude were growth rather than decline, or if invisibility itself had been a strategy. Maybe it was.

Decades later, the art world circled back, as if rediscovering her, but she'd never left. In the late 1980s and 1990s, curators in New York, Tokyo, and Europe began digging through museum and gallery archives, pulling out old photographs, catalogues, and films from her 1960s installations and happenings. Major retrospectives followed, beginning with a 1989 survey in New York and continuing through shows like MoMA's 1998 "Love Forever." Critics who had once ignored her started calling her a missing piece in the story of the avant-garde; one review noted that Kusama had "kept out of sight, ensconced in her own infinite world, but now she's back." Her early work reappeared in major retrospectives, this time with her name attached. The men who had borrowed from her were still canonized, but now, so was she.

In her seventies and eighties, Kusama became a global phenomenon. Her Infinity Rooms toured the world and drew lines that stretched for hours. People waited patiently for thirty seconds inside a mirrored chamber, surrounded by dots, lights, and their own reflection repeating endlessly in every direction. For a moment, they were part of her hallucination, part of her world. Inside, everything looked infinite. No walls. No floor. Only reflections and repetition, small lights blinking like stars, dots stretching toward a horizon that couldn't be seen. People emerged blinking, crying, laughing, saying they felt as if they had disappeared. Kusama had never been clearer (Plate 4).

Museums built entire exhibitions around her. Instagram lit up with selfies. The public called her a star. Critics claimed they'd known it all along. She just smiled and kept working. The attention felt surreal, not because it was new, she'd always imagined recognition, but because it arrived so late and in such strange form. Crowds came to snap mirror selfies and tag her name. Children laughed and pointed at glowing pumpkins. Visitors streamed past her obsessive canvases. The rooms, once quiet, had become curated for spectacle.

She didn't mind the crowds, but she never confused them with understanding. Sometimes she stood at the edge of her own shows, unrecognized, watching people drift through the rooms as if they were funhouses. She didn't interrupt. She just watched. When people asked what her work meant, she gave the same answer: "My art is an expression of my life, particularly of my mental disease." It wasn't a line.

Even as museums called her a genius, she kept the hospital room. She returned each night to a place most would try to leave behind. Fame was flattering, but it didn't undo the years. It didn't heal what had never been acknowledged. What it did mean was that she'd stayed long enough to outlast the silence. In a world that ran on exposure and acclaim, Kusama chose repetition. She didn't trust the fame. She'd stayed too long, seen too much, and been erased too deliberately to believe it would last. She didn't need it to. The work had always been enough.

She still lived in the hospital, walked to her studio each day, and spent her hours painting, sculpting, and writing. Even as her installations toured museums around the world, she almost always stayed in Tokyo, letting curators and assistants travel with the work while she kept to the same walk between ward and studio. Her doctors monitored her closely, though she rarely needed intensive care. What she needed was space. If she stopped making, she unraveled. She once said that creating kept her "from being lost to the universe." The repetition, the ritual, the sheer scale of her work became scaffolding. Without it, the hallucinations grew louder and the self-doubt returned.

Kusama never stopped. She kept showing up in the studio, on the street, in the footnotes of someone else's success. She kept going when the doors were closed, when her work was stolen, and even when she was too sick to leave the hospital, until the world finally turned and faced her. She won by staying, by refusing to vanish, and by building a body of work so massive, so consistent, and so relentlessly her own that even the most dismissive institutions couldn't ignore it forever. Her triumph was endurance. She outlasted them all.

Still working. Still wearing her dots. Some mornings she reached her studio before dawn, made tea, unrolled the canvas, and began. One dot. Then another. She was building something larger than attention, her own universe made of repetition. Her own room shaped by pattern and will. She never needed their invitation. She'd always just invited herself.

I think about her when my own creative life feels overwhelming. Comparison is usually unwise, but with Kusama, sometimes it still helps me to think about what's standing in my way on those tougher days and hold it in my mind alongside what stood in hers for decades.

We like stories about being discovered, about talent finally being recognized. Kusama's story isn't about discovery. It's about refusal. She stayed in the room until no one could pretend she wasn't already there. That's what she leaves us. Not just the dots or the mirrors or the lines wrapped around the block, but the quiet, furious lesson of persistence. The discipline of making the work when no one asks for it. The courage of showing up where they say you don't belong. The stubbornness of building something no one can steal because you never stop adding to it.

So much of being discovered is luck. Staying is different. Kusama made a life out of outlasting the room, standing there in her loudest clothes until it had no choice but to admit she was part of the story all along.

Interlude: Frank Auerbach, Recursive Self-Portrait in Layers

Every day I return to the canvas, and every day it resists me.
I paint the same face over and over, but it never looks right.
I paint the same face over and over, but it never looks right.
The brush drags more with each pass.
I paint the same face over and over, but it never looks right.
The brush drags more with each pass.
It starts to feel like a struggle.
I paint the same face over and over, but it never looks right.
The brush drags more with each pass.
It starts to feel like a struggle.
Nothing fits, nothing holds together.
I paint the same face over and over, but it never looks right.
The brush drags more with each pass.
It starts to feel like a struggle.
Nothing fits, nothing holds together.
I can feel it slipping away, but I can't leave it undone.

I paint the same face over and over, but it never looks right.
The brush drags more with each pass.
It starts to feel like a struggle.
Nothing fits, nothing holds together.
I can feel it slipping away, but I can't leave it undone.
It's not finished.
I won't stop.

Sergei Rachmaninoff

The conductor barely glanced at him backstage. The orchestra tuned, half-hearted and fidgeting, as if they already knew what was coming. Sergei Rachmaninoff stood in the wings, not yet twenty-five, hands shaking. He had staked everything on this night: his first symphony, his future as a composer, the right to call himself something more than a pianist with promise. The audience rustled with polite expectation. He stepped forward, took his seat, and waited for the music to begin.

What followed was worse than he could've imagined.

The piece lurched. Tempos slipped. Dynamics blurred. The conductor, Alexander Glazunov, was rumored to be drunk, disengaged, barely present. Rachmaninoff's careful orchestration turned thick and muddled, but it wasn't just the performance. Something about the piece itself, its sweeping drama, its sharp dissonances, its dark weight, struck listeners as wrong. When it ended, the applause was thin, almost perfunctory. He walked out into the Moscow night, his face blank with disbelief.

The reviews arrived quickly, and they were brutal. César Cui, one of Russia's leading critics, called it a "program symphony" that might have been written by a "conservatory student in hell." Others echoed the cruelty. Some mocked its emotional excess; others dismissed it as forgettable. No one defended it. Rachmaninoff read each review, then shut himself away. He went days without eating and weeks without writing. By the time months dragged on, he spoke only when someone forced the words out of him. He told no one, not even his family, how deep the wound had gone. The public failure unraveled something in him he thought unbreakable. He'd always believed music would save him and now he wondered if it would only expose him.

He stopped composing. Entirely. For three years, nothing.

He tried to write. He sat at the piano with blank scores in front of him, but nothing came. The keys felt foreign under his fingers. He played other composers' music but avoided his own. Anything he had written before the *First Symphony* embarrassed him. Anything he tried to write afterward seemed cursed from the start. Friends told him it was just a setback, but Rachmaninoff didn't believe in setbacks. He believed in omens. He convinced himself the critics had seen something real, something he'd ignored in his own ambition. He began to think of himself not as a composer in crisis, but as a fraud who had finally been found out.

He either slept too much, or not at all. He pulled away from the people he loved. At social gatherings, he barely spoke and at concerts, he slipped out at intermission. The light dimmed in him. He walked the streets alone, collar up, head down. The Moscow winter turned brutal, but he hardly noticed. Failure had settled inside him like a second soul. Privately, he feared he'd wasted his life and that everything he'd worked for had collapsed in a single night.

Still, he showed up at lessons and played well enough to accompany other musicians, but he avoided composing. He told himself there would be time later, that inspiration would return eventually. Each month that passed without music made it harder to believe he had anything left to offer. He didn't talk about it. That was the most Russian thing about him: he kept his suffering hidden, folded under the coat he wore each day. He didn't rage or beg for reassurance. He simply stopped being who he'd been.

He might have stayed there forever if someone hadn't stepped in.

It was his relatives who finally intervened. Watching him sink further into silence, they urged him to see a doctor for hypnosis. The idea sounded absurd. He didn't believe in the power of suggestion. He hardly believed in anything anymore, but he was too tired to resist, and some small part of him still wanted to be saved. Dr. Nikolai Dahl was a neurologist. His method was quiet: a steady voice, structured sessions, with simple phrases repeated until they sank in. At the edge of trance, he told Rachmaninoff the same thing again and again. You will write music. You will begin your concerto. It will be good. It will succeed.

At first, Rachmaninoff bristled. The words felt naive, almost mocking. Yet he kept returning until the sessions became routine. Slowly, something shifted. He stopped waiting for a miracle. He let the words circle, and one day an idea came. It wasn't a finished piece, just a phrase, a scrap of melody that didn't revolt him, so he jotted it down. Then another followed and a shape began to appear. It wasn't the grandiosity of his *First Symphony* but something quieter, more grounded: a piano speaking hesitantly, then with boldness, then finally with certainty. It sounded like a map of what he'd just endured. He worked obsessively, drafting and redrafting, hearing the doctor's voice behind every note. When the concerto was finished, he dedicated it to Dahl.

The Second Piano Concerto premiered in 1901. It was a triumph. Audiences wept. Critics who had scorned him now praised his restraint, his brilliance, his depth. For the first time, he believed them. Yet he didn't feel reborn. He felt patched together, as if stitched with something tougher than pride. The concerto restored him, but it was the *Second Symphony* that made him undeniable. Written over two years and premiered in 1908, it was expansive and sorrowful. Rachmaninoff poured into it everything he had felt since the collapse. The themes swelled, circled back, and rose again. It was music that trusted its own emotion. Critics who once called him sentimental now admired his control. Audiences who once turned away leaned forward. The piece won the Glinka Prize, one of Russia's most prestigious composition awards at the time, and secured his reputation. More than that, it proved that vulnerability, if faced directly, could communicate real power.

Even in triumph, he was wary. Praise, he knew, could collapse as suddenly as it appeared. He remembered the sting of mockery, and he understood now that success wasn't safety. In interviews, he was soft-spoken. In public, reserved. His posture was exact, his smile restrained. The symphony was fervent, but he himself grew ever more contained. Composure became his shield. He'd learned how to survive failure, now he was learning how to withstand success.

He toured relentlessly, conducting and performing, never staying long in one place. He accepted admiration with grace but kept his distance. He rarely spoke of the *First Symphony* again. It remained unpublished in his lifetime. But the Second was different. The Second was what you wrote when you'd nearly disappeared and still managed to return. It faced despair and still kept going. Rachmaninoff never claimed he was healed. What he claimed, in quiet words and careful presence, was that he'd resumed or maybe decided to begin again.

He was forty-four when he left Russia, carrying almost nothing.

It was 1917. The Revolution had begun. Chaos spread like smoke across the country. Food grew scarce and violence filled the streets. The old order collapsed, and with it the institutions that had sustained artists like him. There was no way to pack a lifetime. Only the barest essentials: a few manuscripts, a handful of scores, and the family Bible. He boarded a train with his wife and daughters and didn't look back.

He landed in Scandinavia first, then made his way to the United States. The welcome was formal but cool. To American audiences, he was the great Russian pianist, a novelty, a virtuoso, a technician. They marveled at his playing. To survive, he performed relentlessly. Seventy to eighty concerts a year. The piano was the only constant. He played his own music now and then, but more often Chopin, Beethoven, Liszt. There was comfort in precision, in pieces that promised an ending he already knew.

Composing was different. That required roots, and Rachmaninoff had none. Russia was gone, or at least unreachable. His estate was seized. His letters were censored and the church bells of his childhood silenced. The seasons he used to write by, spring thaw and autumn frost, were gone. The language of his soul drifted further away with each passing tour.

For nearly a decade, he produced almost nothing. People called it silence, but it wasn't that. He hadn't stopped making music. He'd been forced to make a different kind, the kind that paid bills. He smiled through interviews, bowed with grace, but inside he felt hollow and displaced.

He missed home in ways he could barely name. In America, he was a star. Critics called him "the greatest living pianist." His records sold by the thousands and he was celebrated for the melancholy he brought to the keys, but the praise only deepened the ache. He hadn't chosen this life. Revolution had pushed him into it. The world cheered his brilliance without noticing what it cost him.

He missed the composer he'd been, the man who walked Moscow's snowy streets humming themes into the cold, who wrote symphonies that stretched and wept. In America, there was no space for that kind of work. Only rehearsals, trains, hotels, press, performance. He began to think of composition as a younger man's gift, something that belonged to the self he'd lost when he left home. He told interviewers he was "too tired" to compose, that he needed peace to write, but the harder truth was simpler: he wasn't sure there was anything left inside him. The well felt dry. Silence, once chosen, had become a fact. He played anyway. That was what was expected, so each night he straightened his cuffs, walked onstage, and disappeared into the music of others.

Audiences wept. He bowed. Nothing changed.

He was grateful for the career, the security, and the chance to keep performing, but in private he grieved, as though a part of him had been buried. Even in his most rapturous performances there was a shadow behind the brilliance. Not detachment, or boredom, something quieter. A longing for more than admiration. A longing for home.

In his final years, something stirred.

It wasn't sudden or loud, but after decades of near-silence, Rachmaninoff began to compose again. *Rhapsody on a Theme of Paganini* arrived first, in 1934. Audiences expected something somber. What they got was theatrical, wry, full of joy and darkness interwoven. The variations danced and mocked, playful yet haunted. At the center stood the eighteenth variation, slow and luminous, tender enough to stop time. It sounded unlike anything he'd written before yet carried the full weight of what he'd endured. He followed with the *Third Symphony* and later the *Symphonic Dances*, his last work, completed in 1940. It was less mournful than his earlier music, but more layered. Beneath its rhythmic energy lay resignation, memory, and longing. He quoted himself, fragments from the *All-Night Vigil*, gestures from the *Second Symphony*.

He didn't talk much about these pieces. He let them speak for him, but those close to him felt the urgency. His writing had shifted. He knew time was short. Years of touring had drained him, and cancer had already taken hold, though he kept it quiet. His hands, once so sure, trembled when he was away from the piano. Still, he kept playing. He kept composing. He kept beginning again. In these late works, he wasn't trying to reclaim what he'd lost. He was honoring what he'd managed to preserve.

He died in 1943, just days before his seventieth birthday. His last works had already entered the canon. The applause came on time for once, but he hadn't written them for applause. They were offerings. Proof that you can fall apart, lose your country, lose your voice, and still find a way to begin again.

Rachmaninoff never shed the memory of his first failure. He carried it for life, a reminder of where he'd broken and been stitched back together. He rarely mentioned the *First Symphony*, and when he did, it was without bitterness. Just silence, a pause, then a nod, as if to say: yes, that happened and I'm still here.

He worked slowly, cautiously, revising past exhaustion. He never grew careless with his gifts. He never assumed brilliance would return on command. Even at the height of his fame, he stayed meticulous. The early collapse had taught him how quickly the world could turn.

He stopped waiting for confidence to arrive and worked without it when he had to. He'd learned to live with uncertainty. He composed, eventually, not because he trusted success but because he no longer needed to. He'd survived being shattered and he'd found a way forward with the cracks showing. He didn't erase his fall; he folded it into the music, and in doing so, he gave the rest of us permission to do the same.

Not every collapse ends in applause. Some falls draw no audience, no comeback, and no vindication, only the slow work of remembering how to move. We praise perseverance, but not the aftermath, when failure feels final, when silence lingers, when the questions come at night. Was I ever any good? Should I even try again? What if the answer is no? Rachmaninoff's life shows us how to survive that.

His legacy is what he did when brilliance seemed gone. It's the days he sat at the piano with nothing left but habit and muscle memory. It's the mornings he trudged through snow to rehearsals he didn't want to attend. It's the years he wrote nothing at all, and the one quiet morning he began again. He didn't wait until he felt ready or for humiliation to fade. He didn't wait for permission. A patient doctor helped steady him, but no one else could move his hands. At some point, he still had to sit down and, trembling or not, just start. That's the part we forget: beginning again is an act of faith. It's choosing to believe in your own voice, even when you can barely hear it. Even when the last attempt broke you or when you doubt you still can. Begin again.

Most of us, in one way or another, live in the aftermath of something that nearly ended us. A review that cut too deep, a rejection, a betrayal, maybe a silence that stretched too long. The same question always comes: Do I even dare try again?

Some years ago, a project I believed in with my whole heart came to an end. When I'd launched it, around a decade prior, I assumed that I'd found my life's work, and I would never have to wonder about my creative purpose again. When it ended for me, I was devastated. I felt like a failure, sure, but the harder things to contend with were the feelings of despair and directionlessness. I spent the better part of six years half-heartedly wandering from job to job and project to project ostensibly trying to find my next path, but secretly (or maybe not so secretly if you lived in my house), I was convinced that I'd had my shot, I'd failed, and henceforth I was destined to lament what could have been.

If that's where you are now, let me say this as clearly as I can: beginning again doesn't require confidence or any kind of belief in yourself. It only requires movement. Tiny, hesitant, tremulous movement. A note. A sentence. A brushstroke. A plan. A prayer. One small action that proves you're still here. Begin even if it feels absurd. Begin even if you don't know what you're making. Begin even if the last thing you made fell apart in front of everyone. That's the quiet courage Rachmaninoff practiced. Starting from devastation and doubt. From the part of yourself that no longer trusts your own hands. There's no timeline or right way, only the choice: to stay silent or to begin.

And if you do begin again, even if you only let yourself consider it, know that you're not the first person to mistake a collapse for the end. I did too. The world loves to celebrate returns. What it doesn't talk about is the cost. It doesn't say how much it takes to write the second thing after the first one fails. How quiet it is when you work in the aftermath. How lonely. How brave. We like to skip to the comeback, to the triumphant second premiere.

In the aftermath of my shuttered project, my wife, I think as much to get me out of her hair as to try to help with my rolling existential crisis, suggested that, with all this time and space I now had, I finally give writing a real shot. I started without expectation and not quite a year later, I was signing the contract for this book with a supportive team at a fancy publisher. From the outside, I'm sure it looked like overnight success. Suddenly, I was a public figure again, with a big city agent, a respected publisher, and a book that was actually pretty good and all of it had happened, at least in the polished version of the story, almost overnight and certainly by accident. That's not the real story. The real story lives in the quieter days.

It's there before anything actually happens. It's there in the mornings when you sit at the keys, or the canvas, or the page, and wonder what's left. It's there in the first idea you let yourself trust again. The moment your hands move even though the doubt hasn't left. Maybe the thing you built didn't survive. Maybe nobody clapped and now you can't even bring yourself to sit at the piano. That isn't weakness. That's what it feels like to break, but you're still here.

Even if, like me sitting down to write this book, you don't believe in yourself yet, begin anyway. Begin quietly. Begin badly. Begin in fragments. Begin as if you're teaching yourself to speak again. Begin the way people do after being broken.

That's what Rachmaninoff leaves us: not a triumph, but a way back. Not just how to rise, but how to return. I can only say that, when I needed it, I followed it.

Begin again.

Begin again.

Begin again.

Working in the Future's Shadow

Making work no one's ready for yet, hoping the audience catches up before you run out of time.

VIRGINIA WOOLF | GRANT WOOD |
KAZIMIR MALEVICH | CLAUDE DEBUSSY

Virginia Woolf

I didn't come to Virginia Woolf as a literary scholar or as someone training to be a novelist. I found her through the Bloomsbury Group, a loose circle of writers, artists, and thinkers in early twentieth-century London who treated conversation as seriously as any finished work. I met them years before I ever signed a book contract or thought of myself as a writer. When I was building my own multidisciplinary arts project, I studied every creative collective I could find. Bloomsbury stood out. It wasn't just the talent but the constant friction that powered everything they did. Woolf was always present, shaping the conversation but never fully at ease among them. Now, more than a hundred years later, I'm publishing with Bloomsbury Academic. There's a strange symmetry in writing about the group that shaped her, knowing I once borrowed pieces of their blueprint to build something of my own.

The Bloomsbury Group looks romantic from a safe distance. The image of famous names squeezed into rented rooms, arguing late into the night, convinced their art could change everything always glosses over the contradictions underneath. The truth is more complicated. The group's real work happened when the city outside was quiet and the last lamp burned low. Virginia Woolf would sit just outside the heart of the conversation, listening while men argued about politics, philosophy, and beauty. The room would fill with noise, but Woolf noticed most what got left unsaid. She knew how quickly even the boldest circle could close ranks and protect its old assumptions.

From her seat at the edge, she studied every shift in tone and every glance exchanged across the table. Even among supposed radicals, she felt how women were expected to orbit the "real" thinkers. Woolf could see the way the group's freedom was real for some and mostly just an idea for others. She recognized that you could belong and still go unseen. It wasn't that anyone meant to shut her out. The room had been arranged long before she arrived, open for argument but never quite designed for voices like hers.

This kind of exclusion certainly wasn't unique to the Bloomsbury Group. Woolf saw versions of it first in childhood. Her brothers were sent to Cambridge; she was left at home to teach herself from her father's library, brilliant but unofficial, with no degree coming at the end of it. She saw how the same intellect could earn a boy a place at the table while a girl was expected to stay on the margins. She learned the difference between being welcome and being truly seen.

That ache showed up in the pit of her stomach, in the silence that followed when she spoke out of turn, and especially in the tight smile she wore as another idea slipped by without her name on it. Most people eventually learn to ignore it or shape themselves to fit the room, but Woolf never could. She noticed every slight, every time a woman's idea resurfaced as a man's insight, and every time someone decided she was clever but not worth listening to. She kept a mental list. When she felt most invisible, she paid closer attention, looking for the currents everyone else missed.

Woolf wanted to change the shape of the conversation. She wrote with the urgency of someone who knew her invitation could be revoked at any moment. She ignored plot, let memory drift in and out, wrote in moments others overlooked because they were too busy claiming the stage. Call it modernism if you want, but for Woolf it was much more than that. The rules didn't accommodate her experience, so she invented forms that fit. What critics called innovation was simply her way of refusing to disappear.

The old forms could never express what Woolf saw and felt. She knew the familiar way of telling stories, with a beginning, a middle, and an end, but it didn't match her sense of life. She wanted to show

how a thought can echo through a single afternoon, how memory sneaks in around the edges, how a moment can stretch and dissolve. In *Mrs Dalloway*, for example, one ordinary day in London unfolds almost entirely inside her characters' minds; the tolling of Big Ben and the skywriting plane stitch together Clarissa's party preparations, a veteran's flashbacks, and the thoughts of strangers passing on the street so that what matters isn't what happens, but how it feels as it moves through them. In *To the Lighthouse*, a simple dinner scene lingers on glances, unfinished sentences, and shifting impressions, letting us feel the strain in a marriage or a child's resentment without anyone saying it aloud. In her hands, the novel became a living thing. She let the narrative slip into stream of consciousness, let voices overlap and collide, perhaps most noticeably, let silence speak as loudly as any action.

This way of writing unsettled people. Some critics said she was making it too hard to follow. Others accused her of turning her back on what mattered. They wanted novels to reinforce the world as they already knew it. Woolf wanted them to feel what it was like to be outside the spotlight and to be ignored. Modernism, for Woolf, was a necessity that came from her need to claim space that nobody else would give her. By refusing to fit the old template, she made something new not just for herself, but for anyone who had ever felt small in the places where big ideas are supposed to get made. Her refusal spread. Writers who felt boxed out could finally see a way in.

Woolf knew that writing itself was a kind of protest, but she also understood the real barriers that kept women's stories from ever getting told. She'd spent years watching talented women vanish into unpaid labor, family duty, or the slow exhaustion of always being useful to someone else. She never let herself believe talent would be enough. She made it her project to name every barrier and every loss.

Woolf remembered what it felt like to stand at the door of the Cambridge library and be told she couldn't enter without a man's permission. She knew her own small income, that steady £500 a year left by an aunt and later topped up by her writing, gave her freedom most women never had. She could see how money opened doors for her that stayed closed to almost everyone else. She kept track of every way women's ambitions were rerouted, dismissed, or ignored. If a woman was clever, she was called charming. If she was serious, she was warned not to be difficult. Even among supposed equals, Woolf saw women's ideas weighed with suspicion and set aside.

More than just pointing out the problem, she wanted to break the silence that had swallowed generations of women. When she wrote *A Room of One's Own* and *Three Guineas*, she was laying out a set of facts. Women needed money and space to write, but they also needed time, permission, and a sense that their work was worth the trouble. Without those things, talent withers before it can even begin. Woolf wrote for every woman told to wait her turn, to help instead of lead, to watch her own idea applauded in someone else's voice. Her feminism showed in the way she insisted on making space, even when the room itself tried to close around her.

The same sensitivity that let her see what others missed also made her vulnerable. She moved through the world with her nerves exposed, catching slights that others shrugged off, feeling the weight of every room where her presence felt conditional. The work of inventing herself and her art was never separate from the reality of illness, fatigue, and periods when her mind threatened to slip away from her.

Some people wanted to use her breakdowns as proof that she was too fragile for serious work. Others turned her pain into a kind of tragic spectacle, as if the suffering explained her genius somehow. Woolf refused both stories. She wrote honestly about what it meant to be sick, to be exhausted, to be so full of thought you could barely stand it. Her diaries and essays described illness as a fact of her days, something that shaped her time, her language, and the way she moved through the world.

For Woolf, there was no useful separation between body and mind, nor between clarity and collapse. She learned to write around the limits and to work within the uneven rhythms of her own life. Some days she could write for hours. Other days, the effort of holding a thought together left her drained and quiet. What mattered wasn't some myth of genius, but the fact that she kept coming back to the page, no matter how shaky things got.

She worked in the space between what she saw and what the world was willing to see. In *A Room of One's Own*, she wrote that men could "lock up your libraries if you like," but "there is no gate, no lock, no bolt that you can set upon the freedom of my mind." That defiance was the position she occupied each time she faced the page. There were days when even those closest to her missed the force of what she was building. She kept going anyway, guided by a sense that her vision mattered, even if nobody else recognized it. She tore out pages, rewrote sentences, and let ideas circle for months before finding their final form.

Every book felt like a gamble. Even once she had a loyal readership and her novels were keeping the Hogarth Press alive, there was no guarantee that the next experiment would be welcomed. Every new form reminded her she didn't yet have a space she could simply occupy. She invented it, sentence by sentence. She trusted that hunger, even when critics called her difficult or the public shrugged. Woolf knew the real work always happens before anyone cares, when your only company is the work itself.

She came back to her desk, even when doubt was loud and even when the world seemed ready to let her disappear into the background. She refused to stop. She kept building, convinced her work deserved a place whether anyone else said so or not. The cost of seeing so clearly, of fighting so hard for space in a world that wanted her quiet, built up. Her final years were shaped by exhaustion, illness, and the pressure of war closing in on the city and her mind. She wrote about it with the same honesty she brought to everything else. In her last letter, she told her husband that she couldn't go on, that she was hearing voices and she couldn't ruin his life with another collapse.

She walked out of her house, filled her pockets with stones, and stepped into the River Ouse. The world rushed to claim her death as a tragedy that proved genius and madness are twins. That story's easier to tell than facing the complexity she lived. Woolf's death does not erase her achievement or turn her life into a warning. Her work is still here.

The Bloomsbury Group itself didn't last. Even before Woolf's death, the friends had begun to scatter, the world had changed, and the war left nothing untouched. Yet the idea survived. People still gather in cramped rooms, convinced they're inventing something new, hungry for a freedom that's always harder to find than it should be. Sometimes the only sign that anything happened is a name stamped on the spine of a book, or an institution that claims the old energy for itself.

I can't ignore the strange symmetry. My publisher's name calls back to history and offers a real invitation to keep pushing the boundaries. Though not intentionally chosed for this reason, Bloomsbury benefits from a name that stands for a tradition of literary risk, creativity, and reinvention. I doubt anyone in the original circle ever pictured someone like me here, and that's part of what makes this legacy matter. The original group is gone, but the idea of the room is still alive. It remains restless, unfinished, and more open now than it ever was in Woolf's time. I know what it means to try building a space for new voices, and I'm grateful to have a seat in that metaphorical room now, with my name in print on a Bloomsbury spine.

But having a seat at the table doesn't mean the ache of being overlooked ever fully disappears. Before I found my place here, I learned well what it feels like to be invisible, even as my own work moved through the world in other people's hands. The day I opened my mailbox to find a thick, glossy flyer for an art event, I froze. Every word echoed the work I'd spent years fighting for. It was multidisciplinary, shared authorship, creative risk, and it was all dressed up as if this combination were brand new. Some of the folks on the team behind it had been at my table, heard my pitches, maybe even rolled their eyes at my stubbornness. Now my own phrases showed up in their expensive marketing campaign, scrubbed clean and stamped with approval. It's one thing to be unseen. It's another to watch your work walk back into the room wearing someone else's name tag. I know I wasn't the first to have an idea repackaged by someone else as a new discovery, and I won't be the last. In fact, the idea wasn't even mine in the first place, versions of it having existed through the Medici Court, the Lunar Society, the Algonquin Round Table, the Harlem Renaissance, and the School of Paris. Still, presenting this "brand new concept" without me, after I'd spent the last three years trying to bring it to their city, was deflating.

That experience is my most direct link to Woolf's lineage. She understood that being early, or being right, doesn't mean being believed. She knew the world waits for the right messenger, the right name, the right kind of legitimacy before it listens. You can sit in the room, do the work, and still never get seen for what you're really making. The room keeps getting rebuilt, and someone is always waiting for their chance to be heard.

You may know what it is to be present and still unseen, waiting for someone to notice your contributions. Maybe you've spent years building something before anyone around you had the language or the appetite for it. Woolf's path, her hunger, her refusal to accept a smaller life, was never only for herself. Every page she wrote made the old limits harder to defend.

Woolf understood that waiting for permission is its own trap. What you need is the stubbornness to keep working before anyone is ready for it. The rooms change, the rules keep moving, and the hunger never really goes away. Woolf's real legacy is the example of beginning before anyone is watching. The work starts when you're still unseen, and sometimes, that's the only way anything new gets made.

An Open Letter to Grant Wood

Dear Grant,

It only takes a single moment,
a single painting,
for a world that doesn't know you
to demand the whole story.

And when *American Gothic*
swept through every parlor and paper,
when the pitchfork
and those unforgiving faces
became the mask of a nation—

did you feel the cage close around you?

Did you hear them
scratching at your walls,
those voices hungry to know?

History only remembers the story
they wanted all along:
the quiet Iowa man,
steeped in simple values,
capturing a wholesome truth.

But you and I both know
the lie they were telling.

They wanted
an icon,
a symbol

of strength,
of land,
of home.

And so
they stripped you bare,
then tossed six hundred dollars
on the nightstand,

as if that was enough,
as if that could make them clean.

They never cared
who you really were.
The unmarried man,
soft-spoken,
delicate in body and spirit—
too gentle, they whispered,
too strange.

And when they found your truth,
they punished you for it—
not with prisons or pyres,
but with the quiet violence
of questions,

of eyes
that lingered too long,
of doors
quietly closed,

as though your name
was something
they couldn't afford to hear.

Dear Grant,

I wish I could tell you
it gets better.
That the world
eventually learns
to stop tearing people apart.

But we both know better.

What I can tell you is this:

Your truth endures—
not in the silence
they demanded,
but in the defiance
of every artist
who refuses to hide,

in the courage
of every voice
that speaks
where you could not,

in brushstrokes
that soften the edges
of a hard place to live,
in tenderness
that survives
where no one expects it.

And Grant,

your truth
outlasts them.

The ones who stripped you bare
are nothing but dust now,
while your work
still stands—

unyielding,
unbroken,
speaking louder
than they ever could.

And in every glance
at the faces you painted,
someone wonders
who you were.

And in that wondering,
the pieces of you
they tried to erase
find their way
back into the light.

Dear Grant,

you didn't build the cage.
But you proved
they could never lock you inside it.

And now,
you
are finally free.

Interlude: Artist Statement by Kazimir Malevich

Redacted by the Regime, 1928

I am creating [redacted]—
[redacted] art.
I have obliterated [redacted].
Gone are the chains of [redacted].
I have created [redacted].
No saints. No peasants.
No [redacted].
A world without objects.
A world without [redacted].
It is the final shape.
The absolute [redacted].
The black square is not the end.
It is [redacted].
[redacted]
This is not decoration.
It is [redacted].

It is the zero of [redacted].
The [redacted] of pure feeling.
They will say it means nothing.
They will say it is dangerous.
They will say it is [redacted].
[redacted]
They will strip it from the walls.
Replace it with [redacted],
[redacted],
[redacted].
They will say the people want truth—
but only the truth they can [redacted].
They will ask me to explain.
They will say I must be clearer.
They will say
I must return to the figure.
They will say
I must return to [redacted].
They will take my students.
They will call Suprematism
[redacted].
They will call me
[redacted].
[redacted].
[redacted].
They will ask for realism.
They will ask for obedience.
They will ask for
[redacted].
I gave them
what I had left.
I painted peasants
with [redacted].

[redacted]
They hung them anyway.
They said I was free.
But they erased my voice
[redacted].
[redacted]
I signed what they placed before me.
But I did not [redacted] what I said.
[redacted]
I am
not
[redacted]
I
[redacted]

Plate 1 *Caravaggio,* The Incredulity of Saint Thomas, *c. 1601–1602. Oil on canvas. Private collection, Florence, Italy. Artwork in the public domain. Photograph by Reinhard Fuchs via Wikimedia Commons, licensed under Creative Commons Attribution-ShareAlike 4.0 International.*

Plate 2 *Ilya Repin,* Portrait of Modest Mussorgsky, *1881. Oil on canvas. State Tretyakov Gallery, Moscow. Artwork in the public domain. Photograph by Pierre André Leclercq via Wikimedia Commons, licensed under Creative Commons Attribution-ShareAlike 4.0 International.*

Plate 3 *Francisco de Goya,* Saturn Devouring His Son, *c. 1819–1823. Oil mural transferred to canvas. Museo Nacional del Prado, Madrid. Public domain. Image via Wikimedia Commons.*

Plate 4 *Yayoi Kusama,* Narcissus Garden, *installation at the National Gallery of Victoria. Photograph by neonluxe via Wikimedia Commons, licensed under Creative Commons Attribution-ShareAlike 2.0 Generic.*

Plate 5 *Edvard Munch,* The Scream, *1893. Oil, tempera, and pastel on cardboard, 91 × 73 cm. National Museum of Norway, Oslo. Public domain. Photograph by Mariordo (Mario Roberto Durán Ortiz) via Wikimedia Commons, licensed under Creative Commons Attribution-ShareAlike 4.0 International.*

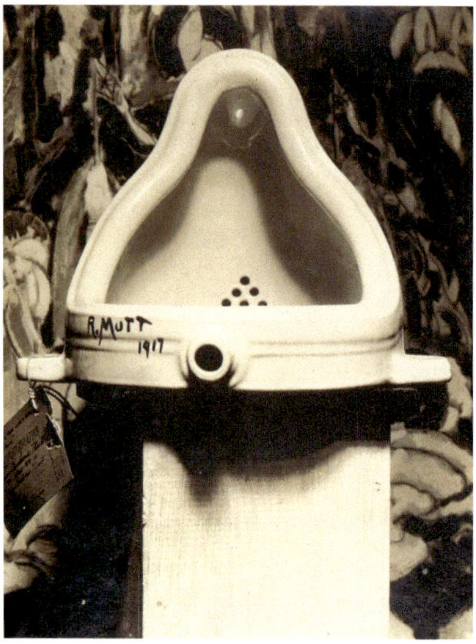

Plate 6 *Marcel Duchamp,* Fountain *(replica). Porcelain urinal with signature "R. Mutt, 1917," on display at the Tate Modern, London. Photograph by Suntooooth via Wikimedia Commons, licensed under Creative Commons Attribution-ShareAlike 4.0 International.*

Plate 7 *Georgia O'Keeffe,* Early Abstraction, *1915. Charcoal on paper. Milwaukee Art Museum. Public domain (U.S., published before January 1, 1930). Photograph by Viriditas, via Wikimedia Commons.*

Plate 8 *Georgia O'Keeffe,* Red Cannas, *1919. Watercolor. Public domain (U.S., published before January 1, 1930).*

Plate 9 *Georgia O'Keeffe,* Oriental Poppies, *1927. Public domain (U.S., published before January 1, 1930). Photograph by Biruitorul, via Wikimedia Commons.*

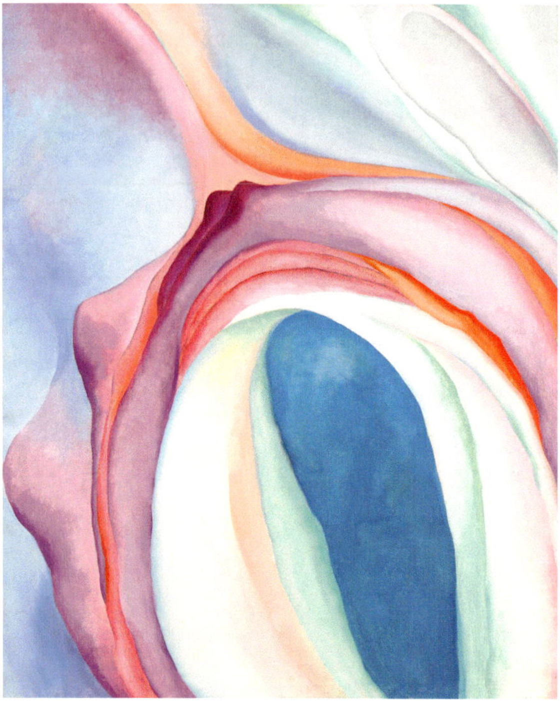

Plate 10 *Georgia O'Keeffe,* Music, Pink and Blue No. 2, *1918. Whitney Museum of American Art. Public domain (U.S., published before January 1, 1930). Image courtesy of Scala Archives.*

Plate 11 *Georgia O'Keeffe,* Lake George Reflection, *c. 1921–1922. Oil on canvas. Public domain (U.S., published before January 1, 1930). Photograph by Kaldari, via Wikimedia Commons.*

Claude Debussy

It's as if he's trying to make music that sounds like nothing at all.

PIERRE LALO, MUSIC CRITIC, 1902

That's what they heard the first time. What they heard was fog. Music that didn't move toward anything. *Pelléas et Mélisande* didn't sound like opera. Not French opera. Not German opera. It didn't sound like anything, and for some critics, that was the problem. Claude Debussy had spent ten years on it, drafting, revising, pulling back, paring down, and when it premiered, many didn't hear boldness. They heard absence. The voices drifted and the orchestra murmured. Instead of big arias that stopped the story so a singer could pour out feeling, the vocal lines stayed close to speech, slipping in and out of ordinary conversation. The orchestra rarely surged over them. It hovered underneath in small colors and fragments, more atmosphere than accompaniment. There were almost no tunes an audience could hum on the way home, no grand choruses where everyone onstage turned to face the crowd. Themes shimmered in and out like heat. To some, it sounded like Debussy had removed everything important and left only the silence behind. To listeners who had been taught that drama required escalation and that genius required weight, it felt like the floor had dropped out from under their feet.

Some of the harshest reviews came from critics who weren't hacks or ideologues. They were intelligent, well-trained, thoughtful peers and colleagues. They simply couldn't hear what Debussy had built because it didn't match what they'd been trained to value. That's the thing about invention; it always looks like emptiness at first. If people know how to describe it, it probably isn't new. In *Pelléas et Mélisande*, the voices move almost like speech, rising and falling in short, plain phrases, while the orchestra stays low and luminous underneath, passing around small fragments of color instead of big, carved melodies. Feelings appear for a bar or two, shimmer, and slip away again. If *Clair de Lune* feels like moonlight catching and disappearing on water, the opera does the same thing on a larger scale. Debussy wasn't trying to impress anyone. He was trying to make sound do something else. He wanted his music to be alive and uncaptured, like breath.

Even the composer Vincent d'Indy, hugely influential and deeply conservative, dismissed Debussy's musical language as "vague and monotonous." Camille Saint-Saëns, one of the most respected French composers of the time, called it "the music of someone who has no ideas and no technique." These weren't fringe voices or fools. They were giants in the field. It wasn't just that Debussy was ahead of his time, it's that his time refused to follow.

He'd trained at the Paris Conservatoire, but he never belonged there. His teachers called him "undisciplined." His harmony professor warned that if Debussy didn't rein himself in, "he would bring disaster on himself and the entire institution." That was the language they used: disaster. As if one student's refusal to obey the rules might infect the building. They weren't entirely wrong about him being a problem. He questioned technique, challenged convention, and pushed back on almost every assignment. He played Bach wrong on purpose and improvised cadenzas that drifted into modes no one taught. Even when he followed instructions, he followed them like a dare. Underneath the rebellion was precision. Debussy worked slowly, methodically, and obsessively. A single piece might take years. He'd write a few measures, step back, and throw them out because they didn't yet feel inevitable.

One colleague described his process as "architectural." Another called it "maddening." He'd revise the same four bars a dozen times, then change the key entirely. He was looking for balance, but also for the thing that hummed just under the surface. He once said that music was "the silence between the notes," and he meant it. It all mattered: every pause, every shift in color, every shimmer of dissonance that refused to resolve. He was crafting something invisible and knew how easy it would be to miss, so he had to make it undeniable. Quietly, carefully, one note at a time.

Impressionism is a term that is badly used. I am not an Impressionist.

CLAUDE DEBUSSY

He hated that label because it missed the point. The name stuck anyway, because critics needed a way to categorize what they didn't understand. Impressionism was already suspicious in the art world, soft, decorative, too feminine, and too French. When applied to music, it was a way of saying "pretty but hollow." It gave audiences permission to ignore the architecture of what Debussy had done. It let them write him off as mood, not method. Once a label takes hold, it becomes nearly impossible to dislodge. Even now, Debussy's name shows up in textbooks as a musical cousin to Monet or Renoir, but he was after distortion. The name confined him, so he rejected it and in doing so, he joined a long tradition of artists misnamed by people who thought they knew better.

Andy Warhol was called a sellout.

Miles Davis was called a traitor.

Philip Glass was called a joke.

Too loud. Too soft. Too far from what they were supposed to be. Misunderstanding disguised as admiration. Praise delivered in the language of dismissal. Even Stravinsky, who would soon scandalize audiences with jagged rhythms and brutal harmonies in works like *The Rite of Spring*, described Debussy's work as "clever pastiche." He thought Debussy was borrowing old tricks and disguising them with new colors. He couldn't hear the rebellion in the restraint. That's what a wrong name does. It doesn't just simplify; it shrinks. It lets people believe they've understood something when they haven't even begun to listen.

Debussy is not a musician at all. He's simply a perfume bottle.

EMMANUEL CHABRIER, COMPOSER AND CONTEMPORARY

That one stung because it wasn't just a critique of style; it was a denial of substance. To Chabrier, Debussy didn't sound serious, he sounded scented. The kind of music you waft, not hear. Other composers dismissed him as ornamental, obscure, or "aimless." The idea that his work lacked structure became so pervasive that a student at the Paris Conservatoire once joked Debussy was "writing music for deaf people." It was a punchline passed around between theory classes, proof that if you couldn't follow the progression, maybe there wasn't one. This is what happens when someone invents a new form. Debussy was no longer treating opera as a chain of arias and showpiece scenes that climbed toward a final explosion; he was writing one continuous, low-lit stream of sound where speech, silence, and orchestra share the same drifting thought. People trained in the old system can't see it, not because they're unintelligent, but because they were still listening for the old signs of greatness, but those were the things he'd deliberately taken away.

Psychologists call this functional fixedness: the inability to imagine an object serving any purpose beyond its usual one. Karl Duncker's famous "candle problem" illustrates it. Give someone a candle, a box of thumbtacks, and a book of matches, and ask them to mount the candle on the wall so it won't drip wax on the table. Most people try tacking the candle itself to the wall or melting it to stick, but the real solution is to use the box as a shelf. Empty it, tack it up, set the candle inside. But few think to treat the box as anything other than a container.

That's what happened with Debussy. He was using the box differently, and it's why even brilliant composers like Tchaikovsky dismissed him. The rules they had mastered blinded them to the possibilities. They weren't alone. History is full of great minds who couldn't recognize what was coming:

- Fats Waller, on bebop: "It sounds like somebody's trying to blow up a horn."
- Virginia Woolf, on Joyce's *Ulysses*: "An illiterate, underbred book."
- H. G. Wells, on Orson Welles's *Citizen Kane*: "A film told by a well-intentioned juvenile."

Even some of the greatest artists could only see as far as their own frames, but not every artist was bound by the same one. Debussy reached beyond European form. When he first heard Javanese gamelan music at the 1889 Exposition Universelle in Paris, it stunned him because it revealed another way forward. A gamelan is a whole room of sound: rows of gongs, metal-keyed instruments, and drums tuned as a single instrument, played in overlapping patterns. Here was music built on shimmering cycles, interlocking rhythms, pentatonic modes; no harmony in the Western sense, no drive to resolve. It didn't follow the rules he'd been taught, and it didn't need to. It moved differently, shimmering without rush, showing that beauty could spiral instead of climb.

He listened carefully. What he heard changed him.

To others, the gamelan was a curiosity, a spectacle from the colonies. Background music for a fantasy of the foreign. Debussy heard structure. He heard time itself arranged differently, and he realized music could be texture without narrative.

This wasn't the only voice ignored by the conservatory mindset. Lili Boulanger, the first woman to win the Prix de Rome, a prestigious French state prize that sent young artists to study in Rome, composed haunting, harmonically rich works that many dismissed as "sensitive" and "fragile." Critics wrote about her health more than her music. Clara Schumann, who performed across Europe, had her compositions sidelined in favor of her husband's legacy. She was respected as a pianist. But her writing? They called it domestic, emotional, not serious enough. It wasn't that these artists lacked clarity. It was that they didn't sound like what those in power had already decided was genius, so they were left out of the canon they helped to shape.

Debussy echoed them. He saw the rules more clearly because he stepped outside them. He saw that misunderstanding wasn't a mistake; it was a pattern. When you make something new, the first thing they'll do is assume you don't know what you're doing. The second is pretend they never doubted you at all.

Works of art make rules; rules do not make works of art.

CLAUDE DEBUSSY

He didn't mean it as a provocation. It was just true. Rules could describe what had already been done. They couldn't predict what came next. Debussy was building something that obeyed its own gravity. He understood harmonic theory better than most of the composers who criticized him, and that's why he knew exactly how to bend it. He was deliberate, and to those who thought innovation meant chaos, that was the scariest possibility of all: that the quiet was intentional.

There's a reason early critics called his music "fog." It drifted and shimmered. It never landed where they thought it would. That doesn't mean that it lacked a destination. It just refused to travel the roads they had memorized. This is what happens when someone invents not just new answers but new questions. The ones trained to know best are often the last to understand, because the sharper your training, the deeper your ruts. Even Mahler, for all his vision, told a friend that Debussy's music "created the impression of being written by someone who has not quite learned the basics of composition." This from a man who would himself be misunderstood until long after his death. It's not always the critics who get it wrong. Sometimes it's the revolutionaries themselves, so tethered to their own innovations that they can't recognize the next one. Having one big idea and executing it brilliantly isn't a flaw. The trouble comes when that idea becomes the only frame they trust. Art often doesn't progress in consensus. It lurches forward because someone got tired of what it used to be.

Debussy knew they couldn't hear it yet, and he didn't try to convince them. He just kept writing. He reshaped the air until it sounded like something he hadn't heard before and until it felt like something that didn't yet have a name. That's what makes the difference: the belief that what you're making matters, even if no one else can hear it yet. History doesn't promise understanding. Some of the most important voices were ignored in their own time because the world refused to listen. Debussy wasn't one of those. He was heard and published. He was performed. He just wasn't understood, and he didn't flinch from that.

When he died, Stravinsky praised him. Ravel bowed his head. Saint-Saëns, who once called his work "sickly and perverse," spoke of him warmly. The shift didn't come from a deeper understanding of the music; it came from the recognition that they couldn't stop it. The sound had already taken root, and it kept growing.

You can hear him everywhere now.

In concert halls, yes, but also in movies, in pop, in the slow underscoring of prestige television. In the tonal palette of ambient soundtracks and the blurred chords of lo-fi playlists. His fingerprints are in Hans Zimmer's atmosphere, in Ryuichi Sakamoto's meditations, in Hildur Guðnadóttir's haunted strings, even in Radiohead's suspended harmonies. The influence isn't always conscious, but it doesn't have to be. Debussy shifted the available frequencies. Once you've heard how stillness can shimmer, how silence can bend, it becomes part of what music is allowed to do. When he wrote *Clair de Lune*, it wasn't the overused symbol it is now. It was radical. A piece that moved like moonlight, soft, indirect, impossible to hold. Now it's so familiar that we use it in commercials to signal peace. That's how fully his vocabulary has become everyone's.

That familiarity doesn't mean he was safe. It just means he won.

He never explained his vision. He just kept writing, and the world, slowly, adjusted its ears. That's the quiet power of lasting influence: the patient reshaping of what people think is possible. He endured misunderstanding, worked through praise that missed the point and criticism that cut too close, resisted the urge to defend himself, and stayed with the work. The refusal to conform isn't a pose; it's a practice. It takes years, and more than a few failures. Above all, it takes the willingness to make something no one else yet recognizes as art.

That doesn't just apply to Debussy.

When Pauline Kael first reviewed *Bonnie and Clyde*, she was told she didn't understand movies. When *Abbey Road* came out, one critic called it "a waste of talent." When Zola saw Monet's early work, he said it was "ruined by feverish brushstrokes." When Chaplin heard talkies, he said they'd destroy cinema. Even giants trip over what's next.

So if you're making something that no one gets yet,

If your work is too soft, too strange, too small to register,

If the silence after you speak feels endless,

Don't confuse that with failure. It might be the sound of refusal. And sometimes, that's how refusal sounds before anyone has words for what you've made. They won't always tell you they don't understand. Sometimes they'll praise the wrong thing. Sometimes they'll nod politely and move on. Sometimes they'll offer advice that flattens everything about your work that makes it yours. Sometimes they'll ask if you've ever considered doing it more like someone else. And if you're not careful, you'll start to believe them. You'll wonder if maybe they're right. Maybe it really is too subtle or too fragmented.

Too messy.

Too quiet.

Too weird.

Too much.

But listen—

If it doesn't sound like what they've heard before, that doesn't mean it's not music. If it doesn't follow the shape they were taught to expect, that doesn't mean it has no form. And if it doesn't resolve the way they want, that doesn't make it meaningless. Sometimes it just means they can't hear it yet.

You're not the first to be misunderstood or praised in the wrong language. You're not the first to be dismissed by someone who should have known. Debussy was too. He just made the next piece. And the next. And the next.

Even if they miss the point. Even if they miss the whole thing. That's fine. Build something that might be understood later, maybe by someone who needs it more than you'll ever know. If it sounds like nothing they've heard, that may be the point. After all, they said Debussy sounded like nothing at all. Now the whole world hums in his key.

But before that happened, he had to endure the silence of being seen without recognition, the kind that turns applause into dismissal, praise into a pat on the head, and waiting into the slow ache of watching your work dissolve.

That kind of silence is brutal. And familiar.

You don't need a Paris premiere to know what that feels like. Maybe you've read your work out loud and heard only the wrong kind of quiet. Maybe you've shown something that mattered and watched the listener change the subject. Maybe you've left the room after making your best case and wondered if your voice was broken. Maybe you've even started calling yourself "weird" or "niche" or "hard to place." That last one's my favorite. Editors still use it on me all the time. Taking up those labels isn't modesty; it's self-defense. It's what happens when you mistake misunderstanding for a mirror and when you start believing that not being understood must mean you were wrong.

But it doesn't.

Somewhere out there, someone is carrying the same doubt. Someone is wondering whether to keep going and is about to shut the drawer, delete the file, walk away, because they think the silence means they should stop. And maybe your work is the thing that would've told them not to. It doesn't need to reach everyone. Maybe it just needs to reach the right person. That's what persistence is. It's not optimism or delusion. Just the decision to keep faith with the work before anyone else does. Debussy never got certainty. He got the work, and the quiet courage to keep doing it. That may be what you're building now. A sound no one yet knows how to hear.

Keep going.

Someone is listening, even when the room isn't.

And even when it doesn't feel that way, I assure you I am.

Creating from the Wreckage

The kind of art you make after everything else has collapsed.

SUZANNE VALADON | EDVARD MUNCH |
PYOTR ILYICH TCHAIKOVSKY | ANNE SEXTON

Suzanne Valadon

This book might be an exception, but everywhere else we don't usually talk about what it really takes to create when everything is falling apart. There's nothing noble about the darkness. Most of the time it isolates, swallows, or destroys. For Suzanne Valadon, art was what she found when her old world collapsed. She started because, in the middle of everything breaking down, it was the one thing that felt like forward motion. That's what interests me most about her.

Valadon grew up in lower Montmartre, the daughter of an unmarried laundress. The stairwells smelled like soap and coal. The walls were thin enough that you could learn the rhythms of your neighbors without ever seeing their faces. What pressed in on her was the clatter, the constant shortness of money, and the sense that choices were already narrowed. From all of it, she learned that survival meant keeping your head down and finishing the work in front of you.

Even so, she noticed things. The way people moved through the streets. The colors in shop windows at dusk. Which errands mothers trusted children to run and which they kept for themselves. That kind of seeing became its own education, the kind that trains your attention to stay sharp when there's no room to spare.

As a teenager, she joined a traveling circus as an acrobat. It wasn't glamorous, the way we might picture a high-wire act in our collective imaginations, but it offered escape and a brief sense of possibility. She learned the feel of a bar in her hands and the exact moment when a catch becomes a fall. The crowd's hush taught her something about timing and about the difference between performance and panic. Then she fell. The injuries ended her circus career and sent her back to her mother's cramped apartment with no savings, no plan, and a body that hurt in ways she couldn't ignore. There would be no triumphant return to the ring. The lesson was colder and truer. Sometimes survival means starting over from nothing.

With few options, she began modeling for artists. It paid enough to survive and left her long hours to watch hands move across canvas, to listen to arguments about light and form, and to study what caught an artist's attention. She learned the difference between when a painter paused because the composition was wrong and when he paused because he was hesitant about taking a creative risk. She watched how a line gets corrected, how a surface changes under a wash, and how a portrait can be made more flattering with a single decision. She started sketching quietly, at first to pass the time, on scraps with a stub of pencil, sometimes on the back of discarded paper. Over months, her drawings grew more certain. By the time anyone noticed she had gotten good at it, she already knew what she wanted from a blank canvas.

Drawing anchored her. Each sketch was proof that she still existed, even when nobody cared what she saw. In the midst of her greatest struggle, she started making art. Whether it would matter beyond those pages was unknown at the time. The pages piled up, and the habit became a life.

Her childhood had already trained her for a world that wouldn't move out of the way. She never expected help to arrive. She'd grown up watching women work until their hands ached, and she learned early that balance came from choosing a task and finishing it. Looking became a way to claim a little space. Recording what she saw became a way to keep that space from disappearing.

Modeling wasn't designed as a path to authorship, but she treated it like one anyway. She held still for hours, counted out the minutes in her head, and stored the lessons she heard without letting them show on her face. She memorized how a painter blocked in shape and shadow. When a figure settled into a chair or leaned against a bedframe, she took note of that, too. On the canvas, she watched poverty, age, and fatigue disappear, brushed away as if they were smudges instead of facts.

When she picked up a brush, she used whatever materials she could find, painting in the gaps between other people's sessions. Her first works were direct and unsentimental. She painted friends and lovers and her mother and herself. The self-portraits face you without apology. She refused to idealize her features or smooth over her age. At a time when women in art were expected to be beautiful and passive, Valadon stared back and made herself the author.

The women in her paintings smoked in bed, sprawled across unmade sheets, worked, argued, and rested. They made eye contact or refused it with great intention. They took up space in rooms that weren't designed for them. The bodies had weight. She ignored the expectation that the female form had to be purified to be worth looking at. Critics called her crude or unfinished, as if honesty were a flaw. Still, she painted. Once you insist on being visible and keep returning to the canvas, it becomes harder and harder to look away.

The move from model to painter was rare, and for a woman, almost unheard of. Her refusal to slide back into the background unsettled people who preferred women as subjects rather than creators. She understood, though, that gatekeepers aren't convinced by argument alone. They're convinced by the work you bring to the table and, eventually, by your refusal to go away. With each canvas, she made the claim again. I'm here. I'll decide what matters in this frame.

Her paintings carried the grit of her life. They came from every cramped room she'd lived in and every moment she'd been told to keep quiet. She knew beauty isn't found by pretending difficulty isn't an ordinary part of life. She saw no reason to make it look gentler than it is. The complications stayed visible because she put them there and left them there. If a truth made viewers uneasy, that said more about the viewers than the truth.

Look closely at a painting like *The Blue Room* and the rest fall into place. A woman lies where a traditional nude might, but she keeps her clothes and her cigarette, propped against rumpled pillows, belly soft, gaze elsewhere. Patterned fabrics crowd the frame, stripes and florals jostling for attention, while thick dark lines hold the figure in place. The perspective tilts just enough that the room feels slightly off balance, more lived-in than posed. It's not an invitation to admire a body; it's a record of a life mid-thought, a person taking up space on her own terms. That's what her art kept insisting on: that working women, aging women, women who are tired or restless or simply uninterested in performing, are still worth painting.

Recognition was slow. She spent years in obscurity, ignored by critics and overlooked by the salons that liked their winners already chosen. Even as her paintings grew stronger and her vision clearer, she wasn't invited into the rooms where reputations were shaped. She kept working and let the paintings speak for themselves. Their argument was cumulative and unshakable.

In 1894, after too many years without notice, she became the first woman painter admitted to the Société Nationale des Beaux-Arts, the breakaway Paris Salon whose annual exhibition could make a career. Her drawings now hung in the same rooms as the men who had once hired her as a model, in front of critics, dealers, and collectors who had never bothered to learn her name. The recognition was hard won, but it was also conditional. She was welcomed as an exception, not as proof that women suddenly belonged inside the institution. It didn't erase the years she'd painted for herself with no promise of being heard. It didn't change her distrust of the institutions that had once dismissed her. She accepted the honor and went back to work.

Her studio attracted people who understood the cost of honesty. She preferred the company of outsiders to the approval of tastemakers. She kept her distance from salons eager to define her in their own terms and from critics who seemed to enjoy deciding what a woman should be allowed to achieve. The studio was the one place where she could set the rules and break them without apology.

Her legacy is complicated because her story is bound up with that of her son, Maurice Utrillo. She was both mother and mentor. She encouraged him to paint when he was young and adrift. Their shared studio was home to as much conflict as creation. He struggled with addiction and mental illness. She spent years helping him survive while continuing to insist on her own work. Over time, his reputation grew until it overshadowed hers, another example of how history prefers an old narrative like the solitary tortured man. The press liked his chaos, and the world liked that familiar storyline. Hers was harder to categorize.

History is full of women whose accomplishments are obscured by the lives of the men around them. The cost of being first, particularly while female, is often a fight to be seen at all. Valadon made space for her son and for herself, and the world was quicker to reward him. Even so, she changed what was possible for the artists who followed. She showed that you can begin without permission, that you can move from the background into the center, and that you can remain there on your own terms. The doors she pried open didn't swing shut behind her. Other women walked through and kept walking.

Success didn't provide the steady ground it should have. She dealt with poverty and criticism and long stretches of uncertainty. There were weeks when money ran out and weeks when the work felt slow and uncooperative. The loneliness pressed in close, because the effort it takes to keep going is its own form of solitude. The people around her came and went. She painted through fatigue and doubt, not because she expected peace but because she had built a room for herself and needed to keep it filled if she wanted it to hold.

Valadon showed up day after day with no guarantees. She painted when she was tired, when the critics ignored her, and when silence from the salons felt like a verdict. Each canvas was a small act of defiance. It said she still belonged. In the end, staying mattered as much as breaking in. She survived by insisting on her place and filling it with work that bore the mark of her persistence.

Maybe you, too, have always worked at the margins, doing what you can with what you have. It's not just about painting or the art world. It's about refusing to disappear when the world has already decided how small you should be. She carved out space for herself and kept it, even when no one else thought it mattered. That kind of stubbornness is still vital anywhere people are told to wait their turn, to know their place, or to keep quiet. Meaning doesn't wait for permission.

We tell ourselves that the right moment has to arrive before we begin or that someone has to invite us in. Valadon's life cuts through that lie. She worked with what was in front of her and made meaning out of what others overlooked. She didn't wait to be chosen. She chose herself and got to work.

The work may go unseen for a long time, or outlast you in ways you can't predict. Either way, that's not the point. What matters is that you occupy the space you've carved out and keep working in it. Valadon's legacy isn't measured by the number of paintings in a gallery. It lives in the act of insisting on your own presence when the world would rather you stay quiet. Especially then.

Valadon began in wreckage but did not wait for better conditions to create. She worked with what was in front of her, held her place, and left behind paintings that still carry the weight of having been fought for.

Edvard Munch

Edvard Munch knew what death looked like. More than that, he knew what it felt like. That's what he painted. His most controversial early work, *The Sick Child*, shows his sister Sophie on her deathbed. Munch was thirteen when she died. In the painting, her face is pale and faintly green, her body slumped sideways, her red hair falling like a final ember. A grieving figure sits beside her. Maybe their aunt, maybe their father, maybe a nurse. It doesn't matter who. What matters is the grief, and it's hard to look at. The brushstrokes are ragged, blurry, incomplete. Nothing in the frame is still. Critics called it "unfinished," "sloppy," "incompetent." Munch called it memory. "I painted not what I saw," he said, "but what I felt." He kept returning to that painting across four decades, making six versions in total. Each time the details grew more abstract, the outlines dissolved, the edges fuzzier like the memory was fading, but the feeling in it cut deeper and deeper.

When *The Sick Child* first hung in a gallery, critics called it an embarrassment. Years later, when Munch painted it again, they called it brave. The same streaked brushwork once dismissed as amateurish was praised as evocative. What changed was the world's willingness to see pain on canvas and call it art. Munch just kept painting until the world caught up. By the sixth version, his memory of Sophie was hazy, but the ache hadn't faded. He let the forms blur into near-abstraction. The child became less a body and more a presence. The woman beside her, once distinct, became a collapsed shadow. Each version asked the same question: how do you depict a loss that you never finish losing?

That's what Munch wanted art to do, not just express pain but locate it. To trace its shape and say: here. Here's the wound. Where others blurred pain to make it bearable, Munch sharpened it. When they told him to make beauty, he made truth. Not a literal truth, not a record of events, but emotional truth, the kind that presses down behind your ribs when grief arrives suddenly and refuses to leave and the kind that doesn't disappear just because you've been told to move on. Some kinds of pain never leave you. You just learn to live inside them.

Before Munch could even spell the word suffering, he knew its shape. His mother died of tuberculosis when he was five. Sophie died the same way when he was thirteen. One day, she was a girl in the snow with a scarf around her neck, smiling. The next she was a cough behind a door no one would open. The same sickroom returned. So did the same fear and the same vigil, only this time he understood what was coming. He adored Sophie. She'd been the kind one, the bright thread in a home darkened by their mother's death. He followed her like a shadow. After she was gone, he stopped speaking for days. He drew instead, pencil sketches of her face again and again, not to remember her exactly, but to practice holding on to her.

Their father grew erratic and religious to the point of fanaticism. He read scripture aloud at dinner until the younger children cried. He called their losses God's will, but Munch didn't believe in a god who'd steal a child and call it mercy. The house became a cathedral of silence, broken only by coughing. "From the moment of birth," he would later write, "the angels of fear, sorrow, and death stood by my side."

When Munch tried to show pain on canvas, critics called him morbid, but he wasn't trying to be dark. He was trying to be accurate. Maybe the part people couldn't forgive was that he looked at darkness and refused to flinch. He was rejected almost from the beginning. When Munch first exhibited his work in Christiania, the critics were offended. One called his pieces "a disgrace to the art of painting." Another wrote that his style "exposes the nerves, not the soul." He was twenty-two. What they wanted was a landscape you could hang in your sitting room. What Munch gave them was *Melancholy*, a man hunched beside the sea, drowning without water. He gave them *Puberty*, a naked girl on the edge of womanhood, her shadow large and clawed behind her. It wasn't that they didn't understand the work. It's that they did, and it made them uncomfortable.

It wasn't until Berlin that the backlash became legend. In 1892, a solo show of Munch's work opened at the Verein Berliner Künstler. The paintings were confrontational, raw, and openly emotional. A woman screaming. A man slumped in despair. Lovers clinging like drowning people. The reviews were furious. Audiences argued in front of the paintings. One critic claimed the show was "the result of a diseased imagination." After just one week, the exhibition was shut down by vote. Munch called it a triumph. The controversy made him both famous and notorious. He was invited to stay in Berlin, where a group of radical artists embraced his refusal to flatter convention.

He kept painting love and grief and terror over and over, because those were the things he knew best. "I do not paint what the camera sees," he wrote. "I paint what the soul endures." Where other artists used pain for drama, Munch treated it like anatomy. He was trying to chart suffering, organ by organ and memory by memory.

Eventually, the pain caught up with him.

By 1908, Munch was unraveling. The drinking had become constant, and he was hearing voices. He believed strangers were plotting against him and he was convinced his paintings were being stolen or altered. His hands shook so badly he could barely hold a brush. He fought with friends, lovers, even strangers in the street. One night, he fired a revolver in a drunken rage during a fight and the shot tore through his hand, taking part of a finger. He later called it an accident, though he also said the bullet was never meant for anyone else. This wasn't the dramatic suffering the critics had once accused him of performing. This was real deterioration. He admitted himself to a private clinic in Copenhagen. The records call it a rest cure. Munch was treated with regulated meals, fresh air, long walks, and what he called "electrification," likely early forms of electrotherapy and light therapy, still experimental at the time. He was stripped of his paints for months. The nurses watched him constantly. He wrote letters obsessing over how he was perceived, how much of himself was still intact.

"I must learn to live again," he wrote.

He stayed for eight months. When he emerged, he was steadier, and something had clearly shifted. Even his palette changed. The violence in the brushwork gave way to something more reflective. His paintings didn't stop exploring anxiety or death, but they became more distilled and more deliberate. He painted *The Sun*, a vast canvas blazing with gold and radiating lines of light. He painted *The Dance of Life*, where women in white, red, and black circle a male figure caught between joy and sorrow. The themes didn't change, but the precision deepened because he was changed. He'd learned to name his anguish without drowning in it. He wasn't trying to escape the darkness anymore; he was tracing its outline. That clarity gave him back his power.

Edvard Munch painted himself more than forty times because he needed to see what he was becoming. In the early self-portraits, his face is wary, angular, lit by cold light. As the years go on, he becomes more ghost than man. In one, his body fades into a swirl of brown-black shadows. In another, he surrounds himself with a blood-red halo. In the last portrait before his death, he sits in his studio, the paintings around him like silent witnesses. His face is lined and stern. He doesn't smile. Most artists use self-portraits to solidify identity. Munch used them to interrogate it. His body of work becomes a biography in fragments: each version of his face its own weather system, shaped by fear, drink, grief, defiance, solitude. His face was never fixed, because his pain wasn't fixed. It shifted, and refused to stay still. "In my art I attempt to explain life and its meaning to myself," he once said. The self-portraits were attempts at comprehension.

Everyone knows *The Scream* (Plate 5). Almost no one knows where it fits in his body of work. The figure is twisted, mouth gaping, hands pressed to its skull as the sky coils into flame. It's become shorthand for existential dread, and it's been mass-produced on mugs and memes and magnets. When Munch painted it in 1893, it wasn't meant to stand alone. It was one piece of a much larger experiment.

He called the series *The Frieze of Life*. It was a system of paintings more than a collection, a visual cycle of love, anxiety, despair, separation, and death. He painted *The Kiss*, where two lovers merge into a single faceless blur. He painted *Anxiety*, which mirrors *The Scream* almost exactly: same sky, same shoreline, but the figures are blank-eyed and calm on the surface, while coming apart underneath. He painted *Death in the Sickroom*, a reworking of his sister's death scene, with the family frozen around her like statues. The center of the painting is empty. He called *The Frieze of Life* "a poem of life, love, and death." It was a structure or, if you like, a choreography of feeling. If you followed the sequence—*Love*, *Jealousy*, *Ashes*, *The Dance of Life*, *Anxiety*, *Despair*, *Death in the Sickroom*—you could track not just Munch's life, but the way he believed emotion itself moved through the body.

Love came first. Always. But it carried the seed of its undoing. Desire turned to possessiveness. Joy gave way to fear, and fear, unspoken, became illness. He was mapping his own collapse. In *Ashes*, a woman stands with her hands in her hair, staring forward, stunned. Behind her, a man turns his face away, ashamed and retreating. In *The Dance of Life*, women circle a man who looks trapped. The stages are clear: innocence, seduction, then grief. He returned to these states over and over, in different orders, with different emphasis. For Munch, emotional pain was a loop and if he could render it with precision, maybe it would stop being unspeakable. Maybe it would even become legible.

He was building a world where emotion wasn't a moment but a landscape. *The Scream* was the midpoint in a chain reaction. The break after love soured. The echo of loss. He wrote of the moment that inspired it: walking with friends at sunset, suddenly overwhelmed. "The sun began to set," he wrote. "I felt a breath of melancholy. I stood still, deathly tired. Above the blue-black fjord and city hung blood and tongues of fire. I felt a great scream pass through nature."

That's what he captured: not a person screaming, but the scream itself. Disembodied. Inevitable. Unmoored. His canvases were records, not catharsis. If he could render what he felt, maybe it wouldn't have to stay buried and maybe it could live somewhere else. "Without fear and illness," he once said, "my life would have been a boat without a rudder." By his own account, he was guided by grief.

Edvard Munch lived alone for most of his life. He never married. He had love affairs that were passionate, volatile, and short-lived, but they rarely ended well. One left him with the aforementioned bullet wound to the hand. Others ended in letters full of accusation and sorrow. He once wrote, "My fear of life is necessary to me, as is my illness." He believed closeness threatened the clarity he'd fought to maintain. He was offered commissions: portraits, murals, and even decorative works. He turned most of them down. What little he accepted, he twisted into something unrecognizable. His mural for the University of Oslo's Aula building was meant to celebrate enlightenment and science. Instead, he gave them a sun that blazed like judgment over a field of shadowed, barely formed figures. He didn't like being told what to paint. "To paint from the outside is nothing," he wrote. "To paint from the inside is everything."

There were years when he had little income. Museums hesitated to acquire his work. Patrons came and went. He sold paintings, then bought them back, unable to let them go. For a time, he even feared his collectors more than his critics, convinced they wanted control. He wasn't interested in praise if it came at the price of his own clarity. To see pain honestly, Munch believed, you had to keep your distance from comfort, from approval, and even from love.

After fame found him, he still remained apart. In his later years, he retreated to a small estate outside Oslo, where he lived with his paintings. Literally, he hung them in every room, even the bathroom. They aged with him. He repaired the canvases himself when they cracked. While he painted new ones, he talked to the old ones. They were his company. Visitors noted that he rarely made eye contact. He wasn't unkind, just distant. Like he was always looking at something just behind you. By then, he'd been celebrated across Europe. Museums competed to acquire his work, but he wasn't chasing approval. He was still trying to see clearly.

There's a cost to that kind of vision. Munch didn't want to be consoled, he wanted to be honest, and the life he chose, the solitude, the repetition, the obsession with seeing, was the price.

We see Edvard Munch now.

We hang his paintings in national galleries. We preserve the house where he died. We cite his influence on Expressionism, on modern art, and on everything that came after. But do we really see him? *The Scream* is everywhere, turned into emojis and Halloween masks like a punchline. We've made it safe by making it familiar. We've turned Munch into a mood. What gets left out is *The Sick Child*. What gets overlooked are the self-portraits where his face is dissolving. What gets forgotten are the early critics who called his work sick, and the later ones who tried to cure it with praise. Munch needed to be read correctly, not pitied or even praised.

Strip it all away and his legacy is an insistence on building from destruction. He didn't paint the soft version of grief like so many of his peers. He painted the one you're still carrying but can't talk about. He painted the one that sits behind your ribs, the one that twists the moment you try to speak it aloud. He certainly didn't clean it up for us. Now that we claim to see him, we owe him something more than admiration. We owe him the one thing he gave us without flinching. Clarity.

We're taught to hide pain. Make it poetic or manageable. Something worth posting. Munch didn't do that. He didn't believe pain should be swallowed or disguised. He believed it should be shown exactly as it was: sharp, misshapen, inconvenient. What he offers us now is a way to trace the outline of what haunts you. Give it shape and color and you can make it visible. Not because it's beautiful, most of the time it isn't, but because that's how it becomes bearable to witness. Not smaller, maybe, but clearer. Pain, left vague, becomes everything. It fills the whole frame. But pain made precise becomes something else. A shape with edges. A scream that echoes instead of devouring. You just have to be exact. You don't have to romanticize or justify it. You don't have to make it useful or redemptive. Call it what it is. Hold still and let it come into focus.

That's what Munch did over and over again. He painted fear, and love, and guilt, and grief. He wasn't asking us to feel sorry for him. He was asking us to feel something alongside him. To see our own reflection in the ache. That's the real invitation: to stop lying to ourselves about what's inside us. Make pain precise, and maybe, it won't get to own everything. It will just be part of your story. Maybe someone else will recognize it. Maybe that's what we're really doing, leaving marks where others might find us. It doesn't have to be anything other than exact. This is where it broke. This is how it felt. This is what it became.

Pain doesn't disappear when you name it. I've written over and over again about the sudden, violent deaths of my parents. No matter what pop psychology may claim, expression isn't expulsion. I don't feel relieved or unburdened because I talked about the pain, but it does stop shapeshifting and taking over rooms it doesn't belong in. Munch painted his pain as if to say, this is where it lives, so it doesn't get to live everywhere.

Maybe you don't need to be understood by everyone. Maybe you only need to make your pain exact enough that someone else can recognize their own in it. If Munch was right, that's how we keep the worst of it from taking over, not with healing, but with precision.

Pyotr Ilyich Tchaikovsky

In October 1893, Pyotr Ilyich Tchaikovsky stood before an audience in St. Petersburg and conducted the premiere of what would be his final symphony. He called it *Pathétique* and told friends it was "the best thing I ever composed or shall compose." It begins almost imperceptibly, a murmur of sound, and it fades the same way. Between those points lies chaos, memory, heartbreak, and more than one something that cannot be said aloud. It's not so much a triumph as an unraveling. Critics struggled to understand it and so did the public. The symphony was powerful, but unsettling. A week later, Tchaikovsky was dead.

For more than a century, listeners have tried to interpret the *Pathétique*. Some hear resignation, others, a coded confession. Some call it his suicide note, while others insist it was simply a final gesture from a composer still at the height of his powers. If you know what Tchaikovsky was forbidden to admit, you hear something different. You hear a man quietly breaking himself apart and trying to speak in a language that wouldn't destroy him. The truth is there, not in his declarations, but in his disguises.

From the outside, his life looked charmed. Behind the ovations, though, was a man in constant conflict with himself. He was among the first students of the new Saint Petersburg Conservatory. His early works won acclaim. High society welcomed him, and the empire embraced him as a symbol of its cultural refinement. At the conservatory, his career began to take shape, and so did his struggle. The school gave him technique, discipline, and a model for how a composer should present himself, but it also reinforced everything he wished to deny. Russian music was conservative, and Russian society prized restraint, especially in men.

This was the age of the heroic ideal: men defined by endurance, strength, and silence. Art, as the expression of national identity, was expected to embody the same values. A composer's task was to shape feeling without ever losing control. Tchaikovsky's music, with its sweeping melodies and sudden surges of passion, was often judged excessive, even suspect.

Within that rigid framework, he became adept at appearing the proper artist, though privately he buckled under the weight of expectation. He learned how to compose, how to behave, and how to carry his name in public, yet the more he succeeded, the more false he felt. His richest works had to be wrapped in propriety to be tolerated. Even his boldest statements, like *Symphony No. 4* and *Romeo and Juliet*, were coded, their forbidden emotions hidden inside familiar forms. The world wanted beauty without confession, but confession was always there, just below the surface.

Inside, though, he was already splitting apart.

Tchaikovsky knew he was attracted to men by the time he was a teenager. He also knew what that meant in nineteenth-century Russia. Homosexuality wasn't just frowned upon; it was a serious crime. Exposure could bring exile, imprisonment, or the end of everything he had built, so he learned to divide himself. In his youth, there were brief encounters followed by shame, regret, and vows of self-denial. He hoped for a time that music might make him whole. Instead, it became the one place where he could express what he couldn't speak aloud.

In 1877, urged by family and friends, he married Antonina Miliukova, a former student. He persuaded himself that it might work, that marriage might cure him. Within weeks, he knew this was no cure. The union failed on every level: emotional, sexual, practical. He left her and never returned. Later, he admitted, "There is nothing more futile than wanting to be something other than what I am by nature." The only person who ever knew him fully was his younger brother Modest, who was also gay. In letters to him, Tchaikovsky confessed his longings and his loneliness, though even there he often encoded the truth. He could never risk absolute honesty, not even with himself.

There was love in his life, but never without complication. Aleksey Apukhtin, a fellow student at the School of Jurisprudence, carried an open and enduring affection for him. Tchaikovsky admired him, felt drawn to him, but kept his distance. Apukhtin's openness was dangerous. There were other companions, lovers, and confidants. Some lasting, some fleeting. One was his nephew's tutor. Another may have been a young nobleman erased from the official accounts. There was tenderness and sometimes devotion, but rarely safety. Tchaikovsky dreamed of what he called "pure, warm, sincere love between men." He believed it was real, but not survivable in his circumstances.

Then came Nadezhda von Meck. For more than a decade, she and Tchaikovsky exchanged letters almost daily. She was his patron, yes, but also a confidante. Their correspondence ranged from music and philosophy to his deepest insecurities. By her rule, they never met in person; she believed that would ruin the bond. Through these letters, he shared more than he could anywhere else. Yet even here he often turned to metaphor, writing of sorrow in musical terms rather than naming its cause. Even she never saw him whole.

When she cut off their exchange in 1890, citing only vague financial difficulties and "threatening circumstances," he was devastated. The loss was not only financial but emotional, the end of the one relationship where he had felt partly seen. He never heard from her again. In the years that followed, Nadezhda von Meck grew seriously ill, her finances were tangled in disputes with her children, and she died in 1894, only a few months after Tchaikovsky's death. With her departure went his last tether to unguarded intimacy. He was forced once more to translate his truths into safer forms like his music. He learned to hide, and the better he hid, the more praise he received.

In public, he played the role expected of him, charming, sensitive, and deferential. In private, he lived with constant fear. He left no diaries. The letters went into the fire. In public, he taught himself to glance past the men he admired. Even among friends he spoke obliquely of "my inclinations," "my peculiar nature," "the thing I must master." Censorship shaped him from the outside, but self-censorship governed him within. To be discovered was unthinkable.

His professional success depended on performance in more than one sense. Concerts, interviews, and social life all reinforced an image of refinement and decorum. He cultivated the persona of the tragic, sensitive artist, but always in a way that conformed to public expectations. He knew exactly how to move within the limits of acceptability, and while his music revealed his deepest truths, the man himself was painted in the opposite colors.

He was careful about his appearance and his behavior, avoiding displays of emotion or affection that might betray him. He kept friendships with men at a safe distance and cultivated his social circles to ensure his interactions could always be read as innocent camaraderie. He often joked about his own nervousness, but the jokes worked as cover, a way to deflect attention from his vulnerability. His friends, colleagues, and even lovers sensed more than he admitted, yet they understood the need for silence.

His concerts were shaped in the same way. Unlike Verdi or Wagner, whose music could feel overtly personal, Tchaikovsky concealed much more than he revealed. His works were rich in emotion, but they never shouted their secrets. They whispered them in subdued melodies and melancholy harmonies. He couldn't afford to let his feelings break loose unchecked. Each note was weighed, each phrase designed to move the audience without exposing more than he was willing to risk. It was self-preservation, and the cost was immense. He poured his pain into music but never allowed that pain to overflow into public life. His silence was a defense against a world that wouldn't permit him to be fully seen.

In the music, though, another self emerged. You can hear it in the soaring melodies that twist when you least expect it, in the unease that lingers beneath the waltzes, and in the slow movements that ache with longing yet refuse resolution. The beauty was inseparable from the restraint. What mustn't be spoken escaped as music. To his brother, he admitted that he often composed "in order to say what I cannot speak aloud." He could be tender in a cello line, urgent in a violin run, or truthful in a key change. Each movement held back a confession even as it offered it, but the effort exhausted him. The more beloved he became, the more carefully he edited his life.

Officially, Tchaikovsky died of cholera at the age of fifty-three during the 1893 epidemic in St. Petersburg. Yet the circumstances of his illness never quite added up for me. Five days before his death, after attending a play, he dined at a high-profile restaurant where he was a regular. That night, despite his known preference for mineral water and despite the citywide restrictions on unboiled tap water during the outbreak, he is said to have ordered and drunk a glass of it.

Really?

A restaurant of that stature, serving one of Russia's most celebrated artists, would hardly have risked violating public health orders simply to satisfy an eccentric request. When a national figure arrives, you avoid scandal at all costs, don't you? Yet the story holds that the request was met, and the following day he fell violently ill.

The official explanation was cholera, but the timeline was inconsistent with the usual incubation period. His symptoms didn't match the expected pattern. Most striking, he didn't suffer the severe dehydration typical of cholera's final stages. He also refused medical care for days, unusual for a man generally cautious about his health. When doctors were finally summoned, they diagnosed cholera despite never having encountered a case before. At that time, the disease was rare among the upper classes these doctors treated.

Another detail stands out. In 1893, cholera victims were subject to strict isolation because we hadn't yet learned how it spread, Tchaikovsky's body wasn't. His brother's home, where he died, remained open for days as mourners came to pay their respects. That seems like a terrible risk if you believed it was a cholera death.

So, if it wasn't cholera, what was it?

Some historians dismiss the inconsistencies as confusion among witnesses. Others point toward darker possibilities. By then, his relationships with men, long an open secret, risked turning into scandal. He had become involved with the young nephew of an aristocrat. When the boy's uncle found out, he reportedly threatened exposure, perhaps even to the tsar.

Would Alexander III have ordered his death? That seems improbable. The tsar was severe in his views, but tolerated homosexuality in the arts, as long as it stayed hidden. If he'd wished to silence scandal, he likely would have eliminated the accuser rather than the composer whose music was a national emblem.

Which brings us to another theory. According to some, the uncle's anger led to the convening of a Court of Honor, an informal tribunal known to occur in the era and place where peers judged cases of disgrace. If such a gathering occurred, it may have ruled that Tchaikovsky should take his own life to protect both his legacy and the empire's reputation. In this telling, he ingested arsenic, staging the water incident as a cover. It's worth noting that the symptoms described in his final days match arsenic poisoning more closely than cholera.

There's also the possibility that no tribunal met and no one coerced him. Perhaps it was simply the surrender of a man worn down by years of self-editing. He'd given the world everything except the one truth it wouldn't permit. Maybe his end was neither punishment nor cover-up, but exhaustion. Or perhaps it was his last act of control.

The Pathétique ends in silence. It fades like breath leaving the body. It refuses the triumphant close expected of a Russian symphony. Critics at the time were baffled. Why set such sorrow at the heart of beauty? Why end with a whisper instead of a roar? I think they were asking the wrong questions. The symphony was about truth, not about despair. For Tchaikovsky, truth could never be shouted. It had to arrive indirectly, beautiful enough to slip past the guard.

From that vantage, the *Pathétique* was more likely a confession than a suicide note.

He couldn't say, "This is the weight that's crushing me," or "This is what I've lost, what I've hidden, what I've wanted." But he could write it into the strings. He could disguise it with tempo markings and build a final movement where the heartbeat slows, the light fades, and no one stands to applaud because they're still waiting for the real ending that never comes. The real ending was already there. It just wasn't the one they were listening for. Now, more than a century later, musicologists and biographers have begun to acknowledge the personal content behind the symphony. They don't all agree on exactly what it says, but they agree it says something that words could never safely contain for him.

Tchaikovsky's *Pathétique* wasn't the only work where he poured his hidden truths into the music. He did it again and again, weaving his most intimate fears and desires into the fabric of his symphonies, his ballets, and his operas. Consider *Romeo and Juliet*, not just a retelling of Shakespeare's play, but a deeply personal composition that encoded his feelings about love, loss, and the constraints of his life. He built the piece around a collision: the stern, hymn-like opening that suggests duty and judgment, and the famous love theme that arrives later, singing over and against it. That theme swells, strains, and is finally shattered by the very forces that first framed it. It's easy to hear in that arc not only the doomed romance of the characters, but Tchaikovsky's own longing for a love that could never be realized, a private desire that kept meeting the hard wall of his world. The tragedy of the star-crossed lovers was something he understood intimately, though the love he sought was always tempered by the unspoken realities of his existence.

In *Symphony No. 4*, Tchaikovsky explored the theme of fate, using the famous "fate motif" that haunts the entire symphony. It's a relentless, repeating figure, like a force pushing forward, unyielding. I first heard it as an external threat, but it's just as much a reflection of his internal battle with his own limits. The symphony is filled with longing and struggle, but it never reaches the resolution he wanted in life. Instead, it ends in uncertainty, echoing his inability to escape repression and shame.

Even in lighter works, he wrote with a kind of duality: beauty layered over pain. Take the *Serenade for Strings*, often considered one of his most uplifting pieces. The melodies soar, graceful and rich, yet there's an undercurrent of melancholy. Tchaikovsky's ability to let joy and sorrow share the same space was part of his genius. The music allowed for complexity, and it also carried something deeply personal. The melodies were his language. His symphonies and operas were confessions, camouflaged as art. That was always Tchaikovsky's genius. He wrote the life he wasn't allowed.

What are you not allowed to say?

What truth do you tuck between lines, bury under charm, or obscure with metaphor? What part of yourself have you edited so well that even you sometimes forget it's there? Tchaikovsky lived with that silence. He slept beside it and even scored symphonies over it, but he still found a way to speak without speaking. Maybe that kept him alive. It was also part of his sorrow, because even in his most vulnerable work, he couldn't be fully seen. He gave us beauty in code, and now, more than a century later, we listen and call it genius while forgetting the fear that shaped it. He shouldn't have had to encode what was most human about him. He shouldn't have had to spend his life making art that said what the artist wasn't allowed to. He did what he had to do, because his world left him no safer way to speak.

Tchaikovsky couldn't say it plainly. He had to orchestrate his honesty, bury it in structure, and let the music risk what the man could not. That's what still stings in his work. Not just the beauty, but the pressure behind it. The knowledge that truth had to travel disguised in order to survive.

Tchaikovsky spent his life coding his truth into music. He gave us his love, his grief, and his torment, in notes. He asked us to hear what he couldn't speak, to listen to what he wasn't allowed to say. In return, we called him a genius. We lauded his ability to speak across time and across the boundaries of his life, but his truth wasn't fully heard until long after his death. His genius was celebrated, while the world that revered his music refused to acknowledge the life that shaped it. It took decades for scholars and listeners to admit what Tchaikovsky had been saying all along.

What survives in Tchaikovsky is not just beauty, but pressure. The truth is there, but only because he found a form that could carry what his life would not permit him to say aloud.

Anne Sexton

Picture yourself in a small, overheated college auditorium in the late 1960s. The folding chairs are half-broken, the air feels thick, and everyone is pretending not to stare at the woman who's about to read. You came because someone told you Anne Sexton was electric. She's in the hallway now, rehearsing the way you might practice before a job interview, except she's about to pour out pieces of herself for strangers. When she steps to the microphone, something shifts. She's taller than you expected, sharp-featured, with that unmistakable mix of teacher and troublemaker. She smiles, but it's a challenge.

You watch her fingers drum the lectern, rings flashing. She looks at her audience like she knows something about each of us that we would never admit out loud. The room is restless. Students and faculty want to see a poet bleed in real time. She opens her book, and you realize you're holding your breath. This isn't just a poetry reading. It's a kind of high-wire act with no net, and everyone here senses the possibility of a fall.

She starts to read. The words are raw, almost dangerous, and you can feel the crowd leaning in, not sure whether to root for her or brace for impact. Some people laugh at the wrong lines, while others look away, embarrassed by the intimacy she's offering so freely. You get the sense that Anne Sexton isn't here to make anyone comfortable, least of all herself.

As she moves through her poems, the room seems to get smaller. You notice people shifting in their seats, pretending not to be affected, but everyone's watching her. She laughs at her own pain, then pulls you in close with a line that lands like a confession meant only for you. It's thrilling and unsettling at the same time, the way she refuses to build any distance between herself and the crowd. You realize she's not performing. She's trying to be heard by someone, maybe anyone, who'll really listen.

When the reading ends, nobody rushes for the exit. People sit there, dazed, caught between relief and something like awe. You hear someone whisper that she's probably headed to the bar, as if the show isn't really over until she disappears into the night. There's a heaviness in the room, the kind that comes from witnessing something raw and unguarded. You wonder if she feels lighter for having said it all out loud.

Outside, you see her slipping away from the building, coat thrown over one arm and a cigarette already lit. She moves with a kind of defiant grace, waving off the few fans who try to catch her. There's nothing particularly glamorous about the way she walks into the dark. It's ordinary and haunting at once, as if she's practiced this exit a hundred times. You realize you're still thinking about her long after she's gone, carrying her words home with you whether you meant to or not.

You've probably heard it before: writing is supposed to save you. There's this idea, especially with poetry, that putting your pain on the page will set you free. Anne Sexton became the poster child for that myth. She wrote about suicide, motherhood, depression, and desire without blinking, and the world called it bravery. Her poems were treated like roadmaps to redemption, proof that if you confessed everything, you could claw your way back to the light. People wanted to believe that kind of honesty could heal anything. Maybe you've even wanted to believe it yourself.

When you look closer, the story gets messier. Sexton's honesty didn't save her, not in any permanent way. The poems kept coming, but so did the darkness. Every admission on the page seemed to drag another secret out into the open, and each one took something out of her. The applause felt good for a while, but it didn't quiet the noise in her head or fill the gaps left by all the things she couldn't fix. Writing it all down became a ritual, but not a cure.

The world loved her for it, though. Critics praised her courage. Fans clung to her poems like life rafts, convinced that sharing your worst thoughts could somehow turn pain into art, and art into salvation. The myth stuck. Sexton was celebrated as proof that if you just said it all out loud, the darkness would lose its hold. Nobody wanted to admit that sometimes, putting it all on the page could become more of a trap than a way out.

I still see it everywhere. Writers, musicians, even reality TV stars, all selling the idea that radical honesty is its own kind of redemption. The messier the confession, the more we cheer, but nobody talks about the cost, at least not until it's too late. Sexton's legacy became a warning wrapped in an invitation. Come closer, tell your truth, and maybe you'll be saved, or maybe you'll just become another story people can't stop retelling.

The more she wrote, the more she exposed. Each book brought another round of therapy sessions, hospital stays, and broken connections. The writing didn't quiet her mind; if anything, it turned up the volume. Her friends worried, her family walked on eggshells, and she kept reaching for language that would explain the ache inside her. Every time she thought she'd emptied it all onto the page, something darker seemed to take its place.

Those close to her saw the toll it took. Her daughters learned early how to tiptoe around moods that could shift without warning. Friends came to expect the phone ringing in the middle of the night. Therapists and doctors became constants in her orbit. At times, even fellow poets pulled back, unsure how to help someone who seemed determined to dig deeper, no matter the risk. The writing that made her famous didn't protect her from the damage.

Still, she kept going back to the page. It wasn't about bravery, not really. It was more like compulsion, or maybe a kind of hunger. She needed to write the way some people need to confess, hoping that saying the worst things out loud might loosen their grip. Over and over she wrote about suicide, mental illness, motherhood, sex, infidelity, and the parts of a woman's interior life that were supposed to stay hidden. In poems like *Her Kind* and *Wanting to Die*, she put language to urges and shame most people wouldn't admit even in private, much less in a book with her name on the cover. The poems became proof of survival, even on the days when she didn't want to survive at all.

Some nights, it seemed like the only thing holding her together was the promise of another poem. Other nights, the poems felt like proof that she was coming apart. It's easy to romanticize that kind of creative fire, even to pretend it's worth the cost, but the truth is, art this raw can burn through a person long before anyone else sees the smoke. For Sexton, the work never gave back nearly as much as it took.

People loved to say her writing was cathartic, as if every poem worked like therapy, but that had more to do with what we wanted to believe than it did with what was happening to Sexton. She wrote letters to friends, recorded messages for her therapist, and filled notebooks with poems that never left her desk. None of it fixed the hurt that kept coming back. Sometimes it even made things harder. Private pain became public property. She kept reaching for words that might save her, but they always seemed to fall just short.

We can talk about courage and artistry all day, but it's easy to forget the reality underneath. Sexton's life was messy and exhausting, filled with appointments, medications, and days when getting out of bed felt like a bigger victory than any poem. The image of the fearless confessional poet falls apart when you look closer. What's left is a woman trying everything she could think of just to keep going.

You can't ignore the way people wanted more from Sexton every time she stepped into the light. Fans treated her readings like confessions, and every new book felt like a promise that she'd keep letting them in. Her pain became a kind of currency. The applause always asked for another encore. The more she gave, the more was expected, until it was no longer clear what belonged to her and what belonged to everyone else.

Sometimes it seemed like people forgot she was a real person. The line between Anne Sexton, the poet, and Anne Sexton, the woman, got thinner with every poem she shared. Readers wanted the rawness, but they didn't want the mess that came with it. Her family felt the fallout every time a private moment became public. For Sexton, there was no way to separate her life from her work, no way to draw a line the world would respect.

The attention was intense, and much of it was adoring. She won prizes, filled readings, and for a while critics praised the clarity and daring of her voice. But the longer she stayed in public view, the more that attention turned sideways. Critics picked apart her work and her life, sometimes more interested in her diagnosis than her language. People debated whether her poetry was art or just therapy in public. Some called her brave, others called her unstable, but almost everyone treated her as an object lesson. The intimacy she offered meant the audience always felt entitled to more. The price of that kind of honesty was that nothing truly belonged to her anymore. Not her story, not her suffering, not even her silence.

As the years went on, the divide between her public and private life all but disappeared. People wrote to her with their own confessions, hoping she'd answer. Strangers approached her after readings, needing comfort or validation, and she tried to give what she could, but the weight of everyone else's pain started to pile up alongside her own. The poems that once felt like a lifeline quickly demanded more than she had to give.

In the last years of her life, the darkness closed in again. The hospital visits grew more frequent, and her circle of friends grew smaller. She kept writing, but the poems felt heavier and more desperate. Family and friends worried, but nobody knew how to help in a way that would actually change anything. Even her therapist, the person she trusted most, could only watch as she slipped further away. The audience still wanted more poems, but Sexton was running out of things she could survive putting on the page.

On October 4, 1974, Anne Sexton put on her mother's old fur coat, walked into her garage, and started her car. She closed the door behind her and sat there as the carbon monoxide filled the space. She left behind stacks of poems, shelves of awards, and a family still reeling from years of loving someone who hurt so much. Her death was reported in headlines, analyzed by critics, and mourned by readers, but for the people closest to her, it was a grief that never really ended.

After she died, the questions kept coming. People wanted to know if it could have been prevented, or if anyone saw it coming. Some blamed the art, some blamed her illness, and some just wanted a reason that would make sense of the loss. Her daughters inherited not just their mother's legacy, but also the public's curiosity and the unfinished work of trying to understand what drove her. In later years, when allegations of emotional and sexual abuse within the family surfaced, that work became even more complicated, forcing readers and loved ones to weigh the harm she may have caused against the suffering she revealed. For many, Anne Sexton became a cautionary tale about the dangers of living your pain out loud. For those who loved her, the story was never that simple.

Her voice lived on in anthologies, classrooms, and late-night reading sessions. New generations kept finding her work and seeing pieces of their own struggles reflected back. The legend of Anne Sexton, confessional poet, only grew with time, but the mess and the ache she left behind stayed mostly out of sight. It was easier for people to talk about her words than to reckon with what they cost her. It was also easier than asking what they might cost anyone who tries to follow her example.

There's a part of me that still wants to believe in the promise that art can save us, that turning pain into language will set something right. Sexton's story complicates that hope. She gave everything she had to her work, and it was never quite enough. The poems made her famous, but they didn't heal the wounds that never stopped opening. If anything, they made it harder to hide from them. We keep reading her, searching for answers she never found herself.

Sometimes it feels like we ask too much from our artists. We want them to dig deep, to be honest, to hand us their darkness so we can understand our own. Sexton did all of that. Her life reminds us that making art out of pain is never simple, and the audience always walks away with something the artist can't get back. The same struggles that turned Anne Sexton into a legend were also the ones that left her undone.

If you keep reading her poems, you're sharing a burden she couldn't carry on her own. Maybe that's part of what draws us to stories like hers. We see our own fears and longing reflected there, and for a moment, it feels like someone understands, but there's a responsibility in that, too. It matters how we witness the pain of others.

When we look back at Anne Sexton's life, it's tempting to see only the brilliance or only the tragedy, but reality is somewhere in between. Her poems are a record of someone fighting to stay alive in the only way she knew how. They're also a reminder that survival doesn't always look the way we want it to. What remains is complicated. She left behind work that changed people's lives and a story that is anything but simple.

I don't think I'd be writing this book if I hadn't read Anne Sexton. Before I ever thought about turning my own past into stories, I found her poems and saw what it looked like when someone wrote the truth without trying to make it safe. I recognized the violence, the loneliness, and the need to make sense of something that never really gets easier to explain. When I write about my own addiction, my time on the street, the suicides and violent deaths in my family, or the ways I've hurt people I cared about, I'm following a path she cleared for me at great cost. Her work let me stop pretending I was unscarred.

Even now, I wonder if telling these stories helps or just keeps the pain close. I think about the people I've lost, and the damage I've done trying to understand where I come from. There's no comfort in putting everything on the page, only a kind of stubborn honesty that feels necessary if I want to keep going. I watch readers lean in, the same way I leaned into Sexton, looking for answers or absolution. Sometimes I worry that sharing my own darkness is just another way of passing the weight on to someone else.

I tell myself I write about these things so someone else might feel less alone. I want to believe that sharing what hurts can make the world less lonely, at least for someone, but as we saw in Sexton's life, that hope is complicated. The idea that confession brings connection sounds beautiful, but its unintended consequences can be real and sometimes tragic. Sexton's life reminds me that the truth can comfort, but it can also do damage, to the person telling it and to the people who listen.

So, I keep coming back to the same questions. Who does it help, really, when we lay ourselves bare on the page? What does it cost the people we write about, and what does it cost us to keep reopening old wounds for an audience? I think about Sexton's legacy and wonder how much of her suffering was eased by sharing it, and how much was made heavier by being witnessed. These are the questions that stay with me every time I write something that feels too vulnerable to share, and every time I decide to share it anyway.

I don't have easy answers. I know that writing can be a way to survive, but I also know it can expose what you most want to hide. Sexton's poems taught me that honesty is never just about catharsis or confession. It also carries the risk of being misunderstood, of being judged, and of watching your pain become part of someone else's story. I keep writing anyway, hoping it might matter to someone, even if the first person it reaches is me.

If you're still here, maybe you've been carrying something of your own and came looking not for answers, but for a voice willing to name what hurts. Sexton's work did that for me, and I hope some of what I write might do the same for you, but I also hope we remember the cost of bringing these things into the light, and that bearing witness asks something of the listener too.

That's what stays with me at the end of this chapter. It's not an answer, but a reminder. Sexton's life and work show that telling the truth can sustain a person, expose a person, and leave a mark on everyone nearby. The best we can do is try to tell it honestly and leave enough room for other people to survive hearing it. Sometimes the hardest thing is to sit with someone else's truth and let it change you, even in a small way. Her voice remains, and so do the questions.

Legacy on Its Own Terms

When the work outlives its maker and the artist gets the last word anyway.

MARCEL DUCHAMP | AGATHA CHRISTIE | GEORGIA O'KEEFFE | JOSEF STRAUSS

Marcel Duchamp

You don't see it all at once. You can't. The hole in the wooden door is just large enough for one eye. You lean in, not knowing what you're about to witness, and only then do the pieces come into view. A naked woman lies splayed on a bed of twigs. Her arm reaches forward, holding a glowing gas lamp. You can't see her face.

You're looking at Marcel Duchamp's final artwork.

The whole piece is a trap. Not metaphorically, it's a literal trap. A door mounted inside a stone archway where the viewer has no choice but to participate exactly how Duchamp instructs: step forward, bow your head, peer in. The only way to "see" the work is to become complicit in its act of voyeurism. Yet the woman inside, her body oddly posed and her face deliberately obscured, resists being fully known. She is the image, but never the subject.

The scene is uncannily real. Duchamp used actual twigs collected from the countryside. The folds of the woman's dress are carefully sewn, and the woman's skin was cast from a real model, every pore preserved in plaster. The gas lamp even flickers faintly with electricity, but nothing about it feels grounded. The landscape behind her is a painted photograph. The light has no source. The entire tableau feels like a memory of a myth: almost sacred, almost pornographic, entirely unsettling.

For two decades, Duchamp worked on this piece in secret, building a life-sized diorama behind closed doors in his Greenwich

Village studio. He left a detailed manual explaining how it should be assembled after his death including what materials to use, where to place the lighting, and how to mount the peep holes. His close friends had no idea he'd been working on anything. When *Étant donnés* was finally installed in the Philadelphia Museum of Art in 1969, it sparked confusion, admiration, and disgust. Some critics called it a betrayal, others saw it as his final masterpiece, but no one expected it.

It still makes people uncomfortable.

By then, the story was already a well-worn myth. Duchamp had quit art. He was finished. He'd walked away to play chess, turning his back on painting, sculpture, the whole world of galleries and acclaim. He was the one who got out, but that startling final piece didn't come from someone who was done. It came from someone who still needed to be seen, but only on his own terms. *Étant donnés* is a reversal. A final trapdoor that opens after you're sure the story's over.

Duchamp didn't just abandon art, we're told. He renounced it. After a whirlwind decade of provocation, invention, and scandal, he supposedly walked away from the whole thing. No more shows, no more manifestos, no more art, just chess.

That's how the story goes.

The myth has a clean arc. Duchamp burst onto the scene, shook everything up with a urinal and a snow shovel, then burned out or got bored or maybe just got tired of being misunderstood. Either way, he left. Artists like to repeat this story with a mix of envy and awe. It makes him seem ascetic, superior, definitely above it all. Even the people who hate Duchamp use the myth to dismiss him. He wasn't serious. He gave up because he couldn't hack it. Duchamp encouraged it. In interviews, he leaned into the idea that art was a trap he'd escaped. "I am still a victim of chess," he told an interviewer in 1956. "It has all the beauty of art—and much more." A decade earlier, he'd said even more bluntly, "I like living, breathing better than working. . . . I thought to stop altogether, and just breathe. You know: breathe in and breathe out."

Retrospectives in the mid-twentieth century treated him like an early meteor: bright, strange, and quickly gone. His 1963 Pasadena

Art Museum show described him as "retired." Art history textbooks labeled *The Large Glass* as his "last major work." Even biographies cited his move into tournament play as evidence of total withdrawal. Duchamp had outsmarted the game, they said, and then left the table. It was a convenient ending. It just wasn't true. The lie was elegant. He said he wasn't making art. He never said he wasn't doing anything.

In 1917, Marcel Duchamp submitted a porcelain urinal to an art show. The Society of Independent Artists was supposed to be open to everyone. No jury, no gatekeepers. If you paid the entry fee, your work would be shown. Duchamp was on the board, so he knew the rules and how to bend them. He submitted his urinal under a false name: R. Mutt. Turned sideways, signed like an artist's canvas, it was titled *Fountain*. It was rejected (see Plate 6).

The board claimed it wasn't art. Duchamp resigned in protest but never revealed his authorship. The piece disappeared. Only a photograph remains, a collaboration between Duchamp and Alfred Stieglitz, staged before the object was discarded. It's one of the most influential images in the history of modern art. The object itself no longer exists. This wasn't Duchamp giving up, it was Duchamp laying a trap.

Fountain marked the beginning of his invention of the "readymade." A bottle rack, a snow shovel, a bicycle wheel. Mass-produced objects, removed from function and reframed as art. He didn't alter or decorate them. He simply chose them. The point was the idea, he said, not the object. Craft and beauty didn't matter. Originality didn't matter. Duchamp was shifting the question. What makes something art? Who decides? What if you refuse to play by the rules? *The Large Glass, or The Bride Stripped Bare by Her Bachelors, Even*, was something else entirely: sprawling, strange, and even scientific. It took eight years to complete and involved diagrams, mechanical metaphors, chance procedures, and sexual tension rendered in wire and dust between two massive panes of glass. He called it "definitively unfinished." Then he walked away, or so it seemed. The machine had stopped, but something stranger had already begun.

In reality, he moved underground. He began quietly assembling the parts of *Étant donnés*: cutting doors, collecting twigs, wiring lamps, and casting molds. Where *The Large Glass* was theory, *Étant donnés* was theater. One exposed its own inner workings like a failed experiment, while the other hid behind a wall, demanding obedience just to glimpse it. The two works mirror his public and private selves. Both are rigged and rules-based. Both are deeply manipulative. And both may have been shaped by his lifelong interest in higher dimensions. Duchamp read essays on four-dimensional geometry, imagined artworks unfolding in space and time, trying to escape the flatness of what could be seen. He didn't step away from art, he stepped outside it, and when the world looked for him in the usual places, he wasn't there.

But he wasn't gone. The myth of the dropout isn't just neatly packaged. It's useful.

When Duchamp is cast as having quit, *Fountain* was just a stunt. When he's said to have walked away, *Étant donnés* looks like a fluke. Frame him as having given up, no one has to face what he actually did: dismantle the entire framework that defines what art is, what it should look like, and who gets to decide. Museums benefit from the that dismissal. Critics do too. You can teach Duchamp as a moment, not a movement. Slot him in as a rebellious sidebar between Picasso and Pollock. Quote *Fountain*, roll your eyes, move on. As long as Duchamp is remembered as a prankster, you don't have to reckon with the fact that he questioned the foundational terms of the entire industry. No one wants to interrogate the foundation. Not when it's still profitable.

Take the market. Duchamp's original readymades were discarded, lost, or destroyed. Decades later, replicas authorized by Duchamp in the 1960s sell for millions. The irony is brutal. Objects originally selected to resist commodification have become precious and monetized. *Fountain*, created as an anti-object, now has a plaque and a pedestal. One of its replicas sits in the permanent collection of the Tate Modern. Critics wrote him off even as they wrote him in. Clement Greenberg, the high priest of modernist formalism, dismissed Duchamp's conceptual work as a "dead end." Harold Rosenberg called him "the artist who eliminated art." Even the praise came with caveats. Duchamp was called clever, cerebral, iconoclastic, but rarely visionary. Visionaries are supposed to build, and all Duchamp seemed to do was dismantle.

He made it harder to sell things. Harder to explain things or to pin things down. So the institutions did what they always do. They told a more comfortable story. Duchamp had outsmarted the game, they said, and then left the table. That version makes him easier to love, but, more importantly, easier to dismiss. What Duchamp actually did wasn't a prank, or a pause, or a retreat. It was a redefinition, and redefining things makes people nervous.

When Duchamp gets turned into a gimmick or a ghost, it sends a message: this kind of work doesn't count. Conceptual artists are still fighting that assumption. If your work can't be auctioned, mounted, preserved, or explained in a placard, it's not always treated as real. The same goes for performance artists, ephemeral interventions, and socially engaged practice. Anything too fleeting, too strange, or too immaterial gets written off. Duchamp cracked the door open, but the myth that he walked away lets institutions close it right back, and the people who suffer most aren't artists like Duchamp. They're the ones without his advantages.

He could vanish and still be remembered. He had wealth, whiteness, maleness, Frenchness, and fame. There was always going to be a place for him in the archive, but what about the artists who don't get invited into the archive at all? The ones already working outside the frame, or erased precisely because they refused to stay inside it?

Take the Baroness. Elsa von Freytag-Loringhoven was a German Dadaist and performance pioneer, living in New York in the same years Duchamp was. Her sculptures used plumbing parts, bones, street trash, and all kinds of other things. Her body was her medium. She shaved her head, painted her face, and wore tin cans as a bra. She published raw, disjunctive poems and even signed one of her found-object pieces "God." In 1917, the same year *Fountain* appeared, Duchamp wrote a short letter to his sister that some scholars believe suggests she created the piece, not Duchamp. There's no consensus. Duchamp never said for sure, but the fact that the authorship is even in question tells you everything: a radical female artist, forgotten and institutionalized by the 1920s, may have created the most iconic conceptual work of the century, only to be buried by the myth of the man who "invented" it. That's erasure posing as art history, and it doesn't stop with her.

Consider Theresa Hak Kyung Cha. A brilliant interdisciplinary artist and writer whose work challenged language, displacement, and memory, she was murdered in 1982 at the age of thirty-one, just days after her book *Dictee* was published. Her conceptual films and text-based performances are now studied in universities, but her name rarely appears in casual lists of experimental artists. She didn't get a myth.

When Duchamp is treated like a fluke or a dead end, everyone who follows his lineage becomes easier to ignore. Women. Queer artists. Artists of color. Anyone whose work is messy, non-object-based, and uninterested in profit. Anyone who refuses to flatter the institutions that write the narratives. Institutional neglect shapes careers. When you're not taken seriously, you get fewer grants, fewer reviews, and fewer invitations. You start to believe the frame they've put you in. Maybe it wasn't real art. Maybe you were the problem. It's not just a misreading of Duchamp's work. It's a warning to anyone who works that way now. It's easy to forget how radical he was.

I worked in experimental performance for more than a decade. I was ignored, dismissed, mocked, and stolen from. I was criticized for being too strange, too loud, even too commercial, but never the kind of commercial the art world values. Those reactions weren't just tastes or opinions. They had, and still have, consequences. Silence can shape a career as much as praise, and coordinated disregard can be just as violent as attack. The system protects itself. Those who benefit from it will always guard its borders. It's the same hunger we see among the wealthy in America: never satisfied, always willing to support policies to enrich themselves at the expense of the vulnerable. The art world has its own polished version of that same impulse, dressed in taste and theory but no less ruthless in practice.

We live in a world where the line between artist and idea is constantly shifting, where memes are artworks, performances happen on sidewalks, and some of the most vital creative voices use no traditional materials at all, but that world didn't build itself. Duchamp helped clear the ground. He questioned permanence before digital art ever existed. He challenged authorship before remix culture, and he refused the pedestal long before performance artists laid their bodies on the line in protest, ritual, or refusal. He showed that art could rest on intent instead of execution. That a gesture could matter more than a finished product and meaning could even outweigh mastery.

You don't have to like him. You don't even have to agree with him, but you're living in the house he knocked the walls out of, and his impact is still expanding. Meme culture thrives on Duchamp's logic: the idea matters more than the image. An artwork can be endlessly replicated, remixed, altered, and still hold power. TikTok videos that recreate museum paintings, protestors using performance as disruption, virtual installations that vanish when you close your browser: none of these are Duchampian in aesthetic, but all are Duchampian in principle.

Even the rise of AI-generated art carries his fingerprints, though he may also have been as dubious about it as many of us. When the artist is no longer a hand but a prompt, the old frames of authorship, originality, and creativity collapse again. Duchamp asked if choosing an object was enough. Now, if we choose, we can ask if choosing an algorithm is. He made it harder to tell where the artist ends and the idea begins. *Étant donnés*, hidden for decades, is proof that he never stopped making, he just stopped letting people tell him what counted.

That matters because he refused to stay where he was put. He refused the frame, and that refusal keeps making space. If Duchamp taught us anything, it's that breaking the frame is only the beginning. Look at Adrian Piper. A conceptual artist and philosopher, she spent her career making work that asked impossible questions about race, identity, perception, and power. In one piece, she handed out cards to strangers who made racist remarks, politely informing them of their behavior. In another, she inserted herself into spaces where she wasn't expected to belong and filmed what happened. She didn't just make art; she made people uncomfortable in ways they couldn't easily explain away. When the art world began to tokenize her, she left, moved to Berlin, and refused to exhibit in the United States again until her work would be treated with the same seriousness given to her white male peers.

Or David Hammons, whose disdain for the art market became part of his aesthetic. He sold snowballs on the sidewalk in Manhattan, each priced according to size. He once dragged a piece of art outside a gallery and left it in the trash. His performances were interventions, disappearances, street rituals. The work wasn't just hard to buy; it was hard to define. Like Duchamp, he chose objects that weren't supposed to be art. Unlike Duchamp, he chose them to reveal whose value systems were already broken.

Or Tehching Hsieh, whose "One Year Performances" stretched the limits of time, intention, and survival. He lived in a cage without speaking, punched a time clock every hour for 365 days, lived tied to another artist without ever touching them. These were meditations on discipline, solitude, and the prison of time itself. His refusal was spiritual. He called his life the medium.

Or Howardena Pindell, who left behind a prestigious job at MoMA to confront the exclusion she saw from within. Her early works were intricate, abstract, and beautiful: punch-hole dots arranged into color fields, but she grew tired of being silent. In her landmark video *Free, White and 21*, she plays two roles: herself, a Black woman recounting experiences of racism, and a white interviewer who interrupts, denies, and gaslights her subject. The piece is raw, staged, and fully Duchampian in its conceptual force, but it came from pain, not play, and the art world didn't quite know what to do with it.

These are the artists who didn't just break frames. They exposed the ones still hanging. It's not enough to say Duchamp made the future possible. We have to ask who got to inherit it, and who's still being kept out of it.

What's the frame they've handed you? Maybe it's a job title. A family role. A body others think they understand. Maybe it's the way you're described when you're not in the room: gifted, troubled, intense, lazy, promising, difficult. Maybe it's the quiet weight of being underestimated, or the louder weight of being praised for something you never chose. The frame isn't always hostile. Sometimes it looks like recognition or sounds like applause, but it still defines you from the outside in.

Think about the last time you did something that didn't "make sense" inside the frame they had for you. You took the scenic route. You made something no one asked for. You changed your major or ghosted the group chat. You said no, even when yes would have been easier. Maybe no one noticed or, like me, maybe someone mocked it. Maybe it didn't go anywhere visible, but you felt something open up. That was a crack in the frame. Those matter.

Duchamp built his own frame, and then he broke that one too. He created a space he could vanish into, and when he reemerged, it was on his terms just to show that you don't have to accept what people think you are. *Étant donnés* is a final refusal. A light you're not supposed to see and a scene you're not supposed to understand. A life's work hidden behind a wall that no one thought was still being built.

Duchamp understood how badly the art world of his day wanted clear categories and fixed meanings. He answered by refusing to let anyone else decide when the work was finished or what kind of artist he was allowed to be. *Fountain* made the case in public. *Étant donnés* waited behind a door and forced the viewer into complicity. If they still can't understand it, leave them a set of directions for after you're gone – and a peephole.

Agatha Christie

The car was found just after dawn, abandoned above a chalk quarry in Surrey headlights still burning faintly, the battery long dead. Her driver's license and coat lay inside, a suitcase in the back. Tire tracks trailed off toward nothing. The slope looked steep enough to suggest an accident yet deliberate enough to hint at something stranger. Agatha Christie was missing.

By the end of the day, the news had spread. *The Daily Herald* splashed it across its front page. Within forty-eight hours, the *New York Times* picked it up. A mystery novelist vanishing without a trace was irresistible. Reports came in from London, from France, even from a market town in Yorkshire. Readers sent in tips. Police dragged the lake near her home with grappling hooks. Bloodhounds fanned through the countryside. At the quarry, crowds pressed close to watch. Sir Arthur Conan Doyle even handed one of her gloves to a medium. Dorothy L. Sayers wrote to friends about the eerie timing of her own detective novel appearing that week.

Christie was thirty-six. Her mother had died earlier that year and her husband had confessed he was in love with another woman. She kissed her daughter goodnight, walked out the door, and disappeared. For eleven days, no one knew where she was.

Then she was found: safe, registered at a Harrogate hotel under "Mrs. Teresa Neele," borrowing the surname of her husband's mistress. She read newspapers in the lounge and danced in the ballroom at night. When police arrived, she seemed confused. Her husband came to collect her, and no charges were filed. No apology was given. She never spoke publicly about what had happened. Not then, not ever. The most interesting part of the story isn't where she went, it's what she did after she came back.

Most accounts reduce it to something simple: she cracked.

How could she not? Her mother gone, her husband bluntly declaring his love for someone else, her latest book reviewed without enthusiasm. Then the car abandoned by a quarry. What else could it be, if not collapse? Newspapers rushed in with smug certainty. *The Daily Mirror* called her "a pretty woman, tired and bewildered." Others speculated about suicide, hysteria, and manipulation. A few claimed she staged the whole thing for attention or publicity for her underperforming book. When she turned up alive, under another name, sympathy curdled into condescension. Her husband announced she had suffered from amnesia. Doctors proposed half-theories and the press nodded along. A nervous breakdown, they concluded. Embarrassing, but not unexpected of a woman.

Over time, the story became folklore. Biographers approached the disappearance like a cipher waiting to be solved. Then documentaries followed and theories multiplied: revenge, blackout, publicity stunt, cry for help. Always with the same undertone of indulgent scorn. Even now, popular treatments of her life lead with the vanishing. You might have noticed that I opened this chapter with it myself. A recent television film spun the episode into psychological melodrama and hinted at madness. Book jackets crown her the Queen of Crime, but introductions remind us first she was the woman who disappeared and thus the myth persists. I know this is a bit like saying, "It's okay when I did it, because . . ." but what most of those retellings miss is that she didn't shatter. She walked away, and then she rewrote the story.

Christie never explained herself. She wrote no memoir clarifying the eleven days, no confession, no denial, not even a matter-of-fact summary. I respect the hell out of that. In her autobiography, written decades later, she skipped the episode entirely. One chapter closes with her mother's death. The next opens: "So, after illness, came sorrow, despair and heartbreak. There is no need to dwell on it." That was all. Her silence was the point. Instead of explaining, she kept writing. She worked through divorce, through war, through remarriage, and motherhood. She wrote under her own name and under a pseudonym. She wrote about murder, jealousy, injustice, silence, disguise, and if you read closely, the eleven days are everywhere in her fiction.

In *Unfinished Portrait*, published as Mary Westmacott, a woman named Celia wades into the sea, ready to die, until a stranger's conversation pulls her back. It's fiction, but barely. In *The Man in the Brown Suit*, published just months after her return, the heroine fakes her death, disappears, and reinvents herself abroad. In *Five Little Pigs*, Christie built an entire case on the unreliability of memory and the gulf between public judgment and private truth. Sixteen years after a murder, a woman already convicted and sentenced writes to Poirot, asking him to investigate again. The story unfolds in fragments: conflicting recollections, emotional half-truths, silences mistaken for guilt. The truth remained buried because no one wanted to hear it. Christie understood that belief and fact are rarely the same thing. She forced her readers to sit with the discomfort of not knowing which parts they'd gotten wrong.

She gave us Miss Marple, a quiet spinster everyone underestimated, who missed nothing. She gave us Hercule Poirot, a foreigner so exacting he was never quite believed until he laid out the truth. Her characters withheld, misdirected, disappeared, and returned changed. Her books carried a strategy: survival sometimes means not explaining yourself. After all, explanation isn't always freedom. Sometimes it's a trap.

She wrote to reframe, and she did so while being called formulaic, dismissed as middlebrow, even criticized for selling too many books. She never defended herself or corrected the record. She outlasted it. They wanted a confession. She gave them stories. The real-life mystery went unsolved, which was exactly the problem. When answers are withheld, people invent them. Christie's refusal to explain became its own provocation. How dare she leave the world guessing? How dare she not apologize?

So others filled the silence for her. Breakdown. Amnesia. Collapse. Pick a version. What mattered was that each ended with her diminished, shaken, contained, manageable, and the industry benefited. The disappearance gave biographers a hook. It made her life "interesting" in the laziest way. Even publishers leaned on it. One anniversary edition of *The Murder of Roger Ackroyd* used her disappearance as a marketing line. A recent(ish) box set opened not with Poirot or Miss Marple, but with: "Agatha Christie vanished in 1926, leaving behind a nation full of questions."

Christie became not only a mystery writer but a mystery herself, packaged, promoted, and profited from. Her life was reduced to one headline, and her silence became spectacle. Culturally, that made her safer. The image of a woman producing bestseller after bestseller for decades without scandal, without collapse, and without apology was harder to accept. The myth of a single breakdown made her palatable. A brief lapse is easier to forgive than a lifetime of control. That is what's at stake: control. If she didn't lose it, if she didn't falter, then she becomes harder to define and harder to dismiss. Christie didn't need the story they gave her. They did.

When Christie vanished, the public wanted to know why she wouldn't explain herself. That's the part still used against anyone who walks away without leaving a note. Silence unsettles people. Reinvention unsettles them more, especially when it comes from someone expected to be transparent and consumable.

The pattern repeats. When Britney Spears deleted her social media, tabloids speculated about her sanity. When Meghan Markle declined interviews after leaving the royal family, she was called manipulative, ungrateful, and evasive. The language changes, but the expectation stays the same: women who disappear must either collapse or be broken. They must.

Christie's refusal to narrate her disappearance is still treated as a flaw. It's a useful sign that something must have been wrong, but what if it wasn't a glitch? What if it was a boundary? She didn't vanish. She stepped out of reach, and when the world finally caught up to her, she was already moving forward, already writing, already reshaping the story.

The people who suffer are the ones still expected to perform access. They're asked to make their pain palatable, to frame every disappearance as redemption, to turn survival itself into performance. When they refuse, the labels come quickly: cold, unstable, ungrateful. The world struggles with women who refuse to be decoded. Sometimes the most radical act is walking away, then returning without explanation.

Christie outwrote the scandal. She became the most-translated author in the world. Her novels have sold more than two billion copies in over a hundred languages. Her stories have never gone out of print. *The Mousetrap* opened in 1952 and played in London's West End for seventy years. Its only pause came with a global pandemic.

Hercule Poirot has been portrayed by dozens of actors across continents and generations: Charles Laughton, Albert Finney, David Suchet, Kenneth Branagh. There are Japanese manga versions of her mysteries. An Egyptian Poirot. A French Miss Marple. Her work has traveled more freely and lasted longer than almost any other writer of the twentieth century.

There are Agatha Christie festivals in Torquay, Istanbul, Tokyo. Her novels are required reading in schools in Argentina and Sri Lanka. In India, a 2023 film reset *The Sittaford Mystery* in a Himalayan town under snow. In South Korea, *The Mousetrap* continues to run with rotating casts, its themes of guilt, performance, and confinement resonating across languages and decades. Poirot, translated into more than fifty languages, is instantly recognizable even to readers who don't know her name.

She never wrote for the world, yet the world claimed her. She did it without spectacle. No cultivated persona or memoirs of confession. No endless tours. Just a steady stream of narrative intelligence, plot after plot, character after character, delivered with a calm surface that hid how sharp it was. Her influence is everywhere, even in places that don't cite her. Any twist that forces you to rethink a story you thought you knew. Any detective whose mildness hides brilliance. Any writer who lets a quiet woman turn out to be the one who saw it all. She never solved her own mystery. She just kept solving others, and by doing so she proved that legacy isn't about visibility. It's about persistence.

We don't need to solve Agatha Christie. We need to see her clearly, as the woman who came back without permission and without explanation. Her silence was authorship. She understood the power of mystery because she had built her career on it. She knew that sometimes the story that remains unsolved is the one that lasts. She wrote women who were overlooked until they proved otherwise, who knew more than they said, who saw and remembered. She let them win, and she did it while raising a daughter, remarrying, and publishing under another name for the sheer pleasure of it. She refused to let the worst thing that happened to her become the most important. She wrote through damage, and she left behind not only a body of work but a blueprint.

She's not alone. Elena Ferrante uses a pseudonym and has never explained her novels or her life. Toni Morrison refused to translate her work for white readers, saying, "I stood at the border. I stood at the edge. And I claimed it as central." Octavia Butler placed women at the center of the future without apology. Each refused the story the world tried to hand them.

Sinéad O'Connor didn't disappear. She was disappeared. After she tore up a photograph of the Pope on live television and said, "Fight the real enemy," the world turned on her. Crowds booed her and radio stations banned her. She was branded hysterical, unstable, and ungrateful. Sound familiar? No one wanted her reasons. They wanted her to be sorry. Years later, after the church abuse scandals broke, after an apology from her detractors came too late, that same act was hailed as brave, even prophetic, but she hadn't waited for approval. She kept making music and kept telling truths that cost her nearly everything. She reclaimed the story without asking. Christie had shown the way first.

Maybe you've disappeared, too.

Not literally. Maybe just for a while. From a job, a relationship, a version of yourself that no longer made sense. Maybe you stepped back. Left something unread, unfinished, unexplained, because you needed to begin again without spectators. Maybe someone filled in the blanks. Called you fragile or dramatic. Called you cruel. Maybe they needed a mystery, so they made one out of you.

You check into a hotel that asks nothing of you. The hallway is quiet, the sheets are crisp, and the lights are soft and forgiving. You don't tell anyone where you are. You order dinner and let it cool on the tray. You take the longest bath. No one knows you here, and no one expects you to speak. For the first time in days, maybe weeks, nothing presses in because nothing is required. You aren't performing the version of yourself that kept others comfortable. You don't plan your return or worry about what they're saying. You just breathe. You aren't gone. You're just not explainable yet. It is not easy, disappearing, even when it feels necessary. You wonder if people will forget you and move on. That's the trick of it. The fear isn't in being alone. It's in imagining you'll be written out.

Clearing away who others expect you to be isn't the same as vanishing. It's starting with a blank page. There's power in leaving and refusing to explain. Agatha Christie didn't vanish. She stepped outside the frame. She let people look for her while she remembered how to breathe, and when she returned, she didn't give them what they wanted. She gave them what she'd written. You don't owe anyone your origin story. Let them wonder. Disappearance isn't erasure and silence is not weakness. Mystery, on your own terms, can be freedom. Christie never gave the world the answers it demanded. She gave it books. Page after page, sharpened into control.

You don't have to explain the hardest thing you've lived through. Not in a caption or a conversation. Not in your work, unless you choose to. Your silence might be your clearest act of self-respect. So, if you have stepped away, stay gone as long as you need to. When you come back, don't apologize or explain. Don't pick up where you left off. Start somewhere new. You can begin writing under another name or walk back into your life with a different center of gravity. You can speak less, or more, or not at all. You can face the same people knowing they'll never see you the way they once did, and that it isn't your job to correct them.

Maybe the only thing that changes is your relationship with silence. Instead of an injury, let it become a boundary. You sit in a coffee shop where no one knows you. You look out the window and begin a sentence, because you're ready. Just a few words. You write without explaining where you've been or catching anyone up. Someone nearby laughs. A cup touches down on a saucer. The world continues as it always has, but you are different.

That's what re-entry feels like. The quiet fact that you're still here, no longer playing someone else's version of you. You're writing forward. Not resolving the past for another person's comfort but deciding what the next line will be. Christie didn't fill in the blank; she wrote beyond it. She turned it into something else entirely and let that stand.

Begin again with your name, your pen, your own strange plot. Disappear if you must. Then return as the author, not of what happened, but of what comes next. You don't owe anyone an outline. If they insist on a mystery, let it be the one they could never control. Let that be the story that lasts.

Interlude: The Critics Speak, Georgia O'Keeffe Answers

Critical Response to Early Abstraction (Plate 7)
Charcoal drawing interpreted as foreshadowing. Lines described as prophecy, destiny inscribed in graphite, a precursor to the painter she would become.

O'Keeffe
"I found that I could say things with color and shapes that I couldn't say in any other way—things I had no words for."

Critical Response to Red Cannas (Plate 8)
Oil painting identified as sensual, even scandalous. Petals magnified until critics insist they reveal anatomy, provocation, and hidden desire.

O'Keeffe
"Well—I made you take time to look at what I saw and when you took time to really notice my flower you hung all your own associations with flowers on my flower and you write about my flower as if I think and see what you think and see of the flower—and I don't."

Critical Response to Oriental Poppies (Plate 9)
An eruption of orange and black across the canvas. Read as confrontation, as grief, as mortality rendered at monumental scale.

O'Keeffe
"I hate flowers—I paint them because they're cheaper than models and they don't move."

Critical Response to Music, Pink and Blue No. 2 (Plate 10)
Abstract forms said to be symphonic. Critics describe crescendos in paint, chords in color, and rhythm made visible. Interpreted as sensual and spiritual at once.

O'Keeffe
"Music, Pink and Blue came into my head when I was out in the evening walking by the lake. I heard the sound of the music and it made me want to paint it."

Critical Response to Lake George Reflection (Plate 11)
Landscape interpreted as allegory: marriage, exile, retreat. Each ripple of water treated as metaphor.

O'Keeffe
"I had to create an equivalent for what I felt about what I was looking at—not copy it."

Last Word

Critics
Across decades, her work has been read through the same themes: sex, death, transcendence, and exile.

O'Keeffe
"Where I was born and where and how I have lived is unimportant. It is what I have done with where I have been that should be of interest."

An Open Letter to Josef Strauss

Dear Josef,

History plays the absent-minded barfly,
scrawling drunken half-truths
on cocktail napkins, just enough fact
never sacrificing a good story
for something minor like the truth.

Instead

History remembers you as a great man,
Born into Europe's most powerful musical family,
And though reluctant to join the family business,
Ever dutiful and obliging in the end.
You were Austria's favorite son.

While Papa composed for the Royals
and Johann built his orchestra,
no one noticed that you carried a sketch pad
and grease pencils and covered every empty score
with porticos and colonnades and imposing granite arches.

But what hope is there for an architect
when the family business is building symphonies?
So when Papa died and Johann took ill,
you learned how to compose a waltz

History remembers your reluctance.
That first composition aptly titled
Die Ersten und Letzten,
The First and the Last,
Just enough truth to claim
a growing love of composing
eventually swept away
a youthful stubbornness
and you'd accepted your rightful place

History remembers that this is a lie
But plays the absent-minded barfly—
it really does make a good story that way.

Admit it, Josef,
before history
beats you back.
Not love, not fate
Immer verpflichtet.
Always obliged.
You were drunk when the argument started
And those men beat you to death in that bar
steps away from a waiting orchestra.

Josef, you would have made such a wonderful architect.

That same year, 5,000 miles away,
an American boy was born: Joseph Strauss.
They say he dreamed of being an architect.
They say he carried sketch pads and grease pencils,
never knew where the habit came from.
They say when his parents would play the piano

Would tell him that he had a bright future in music
That he would smile—and fill his sketch pad
with porticos and colonnades and imposing granite arches.

There is obligation in his story, too, Josef.
It comes for all of us sooner or later
when it came for this man,
when it came for this Joseph Strauss,
Sixty-three years later and 5,000 miles away
Do you know what he did?
He turned his back on obligation
and he built the Golden Gate Bridge.

Dear Josef,

I am not naïve
I know not every story has a happy ending.
Some dreams die.
but every time it seems easier to give up
than to take another step
I remember that you learned this lesson for all of us
That you became another man.
That you finally built your bridge.

It's why I carry a sketch pad and grease pencils.
It's why I've always believed in trying again.
Because sometimes,
the same soul gets a second chance:
to dream again, to say no,
and to finally build that bridge.

Coda

They were never looking for someone like you. Not really. You were always too much or too little in the wrong ways: too quiet, too intense, too slow, too strange, too sensitive, too loud, too smart where it didn't count, not smart enough where it did. You lived just outside the frame. So they told you, maybe not out loud but in every sideways glance, that your work was extra. Optional. Something that didn't really count.

That's the lie this book came to expose, because this was never just a book about artists. Not really. It's about what happens when you refuse to stick to the script. When you drop the storyline they handed you, you stop playing the role they wrote for you without your consent. You walk offstage mid-scene and keep going, out the side door and into the night. It's about what it costs to be dismissed, mocked, broken, or silenced, and to keep making anyway. It's about how many people they tried to erase, and how many came back sharper, stranger, louder, and more themselves than ever.

That includes you. Don't wait to be picked. Don't wait for credentials, clarity, or some official invitation. The people in these pages weren't chosen. They chose themselves. Most were ignored, ridiculed, betrayed, or punished for what they made, but they kept going, not because they knew it would endure, but because it mattered to them.

Sources and Further Reading

This section includes sources used in the research and writing of this book, organized by chapter. While direct citations are not included in the text, the following works provided historical details, context, and insights that informed the narratives. Readers interested in further exploration can consult these sources.

Caravaggio

Fried, Michael. *The Moment of Caravaggio*. Princeton, NJ: Princeton University Press, 2010.
Langdon, Helen. *Caravaggio: A Life*. New York: Farrar, Straus and Giroux, 1998.
Schütze, Sebastian. *Caravaggio: The Complete Works*. Cologne: Taschen, 2015.

Modest Mussorgsky

Brown, David. *Mussorgsky: His Life and Works*. Oxford: Oxford University Press, 2002.
Calvocoressi, Michel-Dimitri. *Modest Mussorgsky: His Life and Works*. London: Rockliff, 1956.
Emerson, Caryl, and Robert William Oldani. *Modest Mussorgsky and Boris Godunov: Myths, Realities, Reconsiderations*. Cambridge: Cambridge University Press, 1994.

Oscar Wilde

Ellmann, Richard. *Oscar Wilde*. New York: Vintage, 1988.
Frankel, Nicholas. *Oscar Wilde: The Unrepentant Years*. Cambridge, MA: Harvard University Press, 2017.
Holland, Merlin. *Irish Peacock and Scarlet Marquess: The Real Trial of Oscar Wilde*. London: Fourth Estate, 2003.

Frédéric Chopin

Eigeldinger, Jean-Jacques. *Chopin: Pianist and Teacher as Seen by His Pupils*. Cambridge: Cambridge University Press, 1986.
Walker, Alan. *Fryderyk Chopin: A Life and Times*. New York: Farrar, Straus and Giroux, 2018.
Zamoyski, Adam. *Chopin: Prince of the Romantics*. London: Harper Press, 2010.

Pablo Picasso

Cox, Neil. *Cubism*. London: Phaidon, 2000.
Gilot, Françoise, and Carlton Lake. *Life with Picasso*. New York: New York Review Books, 2019.
O'Brian, Patrick. *Pablo Ruiz Picasso: A Biography*. New York: W. W. Norton, 1994.
Richardson, John. *A Life of Picasso*. 3 vols. New York: Alfred A. Knopf, 1991–2007.

James Baldwin

Glaude Jr., Eddie S. *Begin Again: James Baldwin's America and Its Urgent Lessons for Our Own*. New York: Crown, 2020.
Leeming, David. *James Baldwin: A Biography*. New York: Alfred A. Knopf, 1994.
Peck, Raoul. *I Am Not Your Negro*. New York: Vintage, 2017.

Francisco Goya

Hughes, Robert. *Goya*. New York: Alfred A. Knopf, 2003.
Tomlinson, Janis A. *Goya: A Portrait of the Artist*. Princeton, NJ: Princeton University Press, 2020.

Mary Shelley

Groom, Nick. *The Vampire: A New History*. New Haven, CT, and London: Yale University Press, 2018.
Seymour, Miranda. *Mary Shelley*. New York: Grove Press, 2000.
Wolfson, Susan J. *Romantic Interactions: Social Being and the Turns of Literary Action*. Baltimore, MD: Johns Hopkins University Press, 2010.

Dmitri Shostakovich

Fay, Laurel. *Shostakovich: A Life*. Oxford and New York: Oxford University Press, 2000.
Volkov, Solomon. *Testimony: The Memoirs of Dmitri Shostakovich*. New York: Harper & Row, 1979.

Yayoi Kusama

Kusama, Yayoi. *Infinity Net: The Autobiography of Yayoi Kusama*, trans. Ralph McCarthy. London: Tate Publishing, 2015.
Kusama, Yayoi, and Akira Shibutami. *Yayoi Kusama: All About My Love*. London and New York: Thames & Hudson, 2019.
Yoshitake, Mika, ed. *Yayoi Kusama: Infinity Mirrors*. Hirshhorn Museum and Sculpture Garden; Munich: DelMonico Books/Prestel, 2017.

Sergei Rachmaninoff

Bertensson, Sergei, and Jay Leyda. *Sergei Rachmaninoff: A Lifetime in Music*. Bloomington and Indianapolis: Indiana University Press, 2001.

Harrison, Max. *Rachmaninoff: Life, Works, Recordings*. London and New York: Continuum, 2005.
Norris, Geoffrey. *Rachmaninoff*. Oxford: Oxford University Press, 2001.

Virginia Woolf

Acheson, James, ed. *Virginia Woolf*. London: Bloomsbury Academic, 2017.
Caws, Mary Ann, ed. *Bloomsbury and France: Art and Friends*. Oxford: Oxford University Press, 2000.
Goldman, Jane. *The Feminist Aesthetics of Virginia Woolf: Modernism, Post-Impressionism, and the Politics of the Visual*. Cambridge: Cambridge University Press, 1998.
Rosenbaum, Stanford Patrick, ed. *The Bloomsbury Group: A Collection of Memoirs and Commentary*. Toronto: University of Toronto Press, 1995.

Grant Wood

Adams, Henry. *Thomas Hart Benton: An American Original*. New York: Alfred A. Knopf, 1989.
Corn, Wanda M. *Grant Wood: The Regionalist Vision*. New Haven, CT: Yale University Press, 1983.
Dennis, James M. *Grant Wood: A Study in American Art and Culture*. New York: Viking Press, 1975.

Claude Debussy

Tim P. German and Margaret Anne Defeyter. "Immunity to Functional Fixedness in Young Children." *Psychonomic Bulletin & Review* 7, no. 4 (2000): 707–12. doi:10.3758/BF03213010. (Cited in relation to the candle experiment, used as metaphor in this chapter.)
Lockspeiser, Edward. *Debussy: His Life and Mind*, 2 vols. Cambridge and New York: Cambridge University Press, 1978.
Roberts, Paul. *Claude Debussy*. London and New York: Phaidon, 2008.
Trezise, Simon. *The Cambridge Companion to Debussy*. Cambridge: Cambridge University Press, 2003.

Kazimir Malevich

Andersen, Troels. *Kazimir Malevich: Catalogue Raisonné of the Berlin Exhibition 1927*. Amsterdam: Stedelijk Museum, 1970.
Bowlt, John E. *Russian Art of the Avant-Garde: Theory and Criticism, 1902–1934*. Rev. and enl. ed. London: Thames & Hudson, 1988.
McDonald, Alison, and Ealan Wingate, eds. *Malevich and the American Legacy*. New York: Gagosian Gallery, 2011.

Suzanne Valadon

Hewitt, Catherine. *Renoir's Dancer: The Secret Life of Suzanne Valadon*. New York: St. Martin's Press, 2018.
Musée de Montmartre. *Valadon, Utrillo & Utter: The Rue Cortot Studio, 1912–1926*. Paris: Paris Musées, 2015.
Rose, June. *Suzanne Valadon: The Mistress of Montmartre*. London: Richard Cohen Books, 1998.

Edvard Munch

Eggum, Arne. *Edvard Munch: Paintings, Sketches, and Studies*. London: Thames & Hudson, 1984.
Prideaux, Sue. *Edvard Munch: Behind the Scream*. New Haven, CT, and London: Yale University Press, 2005.
Reed, Christopher. *Art and Homosexuality: A History of Ideas*. New York: Oxford University Press, 2011.

Pyotr Ilyich Tchaikovsky

Brown, David. *Tchaikovsky: The Man and His Music*. New York: Pegasus Books, 2007.
Holden, Anthony. *Tchaikovsky: A Biography*. New York: Random House, 1995.
Poznansky, Alexander. *Tchaikovsky: The Quest for the Inner Man*. New York: Schirmer Books, 1991.

Anne Sexton

Middlebrook, Diane Wood. *Anne Sexton: A Biography*. Boston, MA: Houghton Mifflin, 1991.
Sexton, Anne. *The Complete Poems*. Boston, MA: Houghton Mifflin, 1981.
Sexton, Linda Gray. *Searching for Mercy Street: My Journey Back to My Mother, Anne Sexton*. Boston, MA: Little, Brown, 1994.

Marcel Duchamp

Ades, Dawn, Neil Cox, and David Hopkins. *Marcel Duchamp*. New ed. London and New York: Thames & Hudson, 2021.
Cabanne, Pierre. *Dialogues with Marcel Duchamp*. Translated from the French by Ron Padgett. New York: Da Capo Press, 1987.
Tomkins, Calvin. *Duchamp: A Biography*. New York: Henry Holt, 1996.

Agatha Christie

Christie, Agatha. *An Autobiography*. London: Collins, 1977.
Morgan, Janet. *Agatha Christie: A Biography*. New York: Alfred A. Knopf, 1985.
Thompson, Laura. *Agatha Christie: A Mysterious Life*. New York: Pegasus Books, 2018.

Georgia O'Keeffe

Drohojowska-Philp, Hunter. *Full Bloom: The Art and Life of Georgia O'Keeffe*. New York: W.W. Norton, 2004.
O'Keeffe, Georgia. *Georgia O'Keeffe*. New York: Viking Press, 1976.

Josef Strauss

Huscher, Phillip. "*The Strauss Family.*" *Program notes*. Chicago Symphony Orchestra. Rosenthal Archives of the Chicago Symphony Orchestra Association, Chicago.

Wechsberg, Joseph. *The Waltz Emperors: The Life and Times and Music of the Strauss Family*. New York: G. P. Putnam's Sons, 1973.

Wyn Jones, David. *The Strauss Dynasty and Habsburg Vienna*. Cambridge: Cambridge University Press, 2023.

Acknowledgments

It turns out that writing a book is a great deal more difficult than writing a poem, which is where I'd gained most of my writing experience prior to this undertaking. I feel certain it would have been impossible for me to do without the support, sometimes enthusiastic and sometimes begrudging, of a number of unsuspecting victims of my imposition.

My greatest regret is that my parents didn't live to see this book published. While neither was overly generous with compliments in life, they always had high praise for my writing and would have been more thrilled than even I to see it in print. They are acknowledged here along with those other indispensable few.

To My Family

- To my parents, who always hoped this day would come.
- To my learned aunt, who also hoped this day would come, but mostly so I would stop sending her manuscript versions to read.
- To my stepbrother, who has occasionally given me a hard time when I start a company and give myself a title he deems to be above my station. It's "author" now.

To My Collaborators and Colleagues

- To Matthias, my long-time collaborator, for striving to keep me from embarrassing myself: a Herculean task that deserves its own line on his LinkedIn profile.
- To Kevin O'Connor and Krista Van Dolzer, both of whom passed on this manuscript, but not before offering insightful advice and stalwart encouragement about its future.
- To Giles Anderson, my agent, who didn't pass on this manuscript and who, as a result, was forced to earn every single penny of however much I'm paying him to represent me.
- To Jacqueline Flynn, Mikayla Lindsay, and the entire team at Bloomsbury Academic, as well as Janice Braunstein and her production crew for being the right partners to bring this "hard to place" book into the world.
- All others, here unnamed, at Bloomsbury, as well, since one of the awkward realities is that this acknowledgments page has to be finalized before I've met everyone involved.

To the Creatives and the Other Book People Who Helped Get Me Here

- To Cinnamon for believing in me in spite of all existing evidence that she shouldn't.
- To Johnny and Dan, for pulling me in.
- To the Masons, for trying to make me feel welcome enough to stay.
- To Ross and Samantha, for being the angel and devil on my shoulders. No, that doesn't sound right. Devil and devil?
- To everybody else in that small army of hooligan poets who gave me my first taste of literary success. In a way, you did this to yourselves.

- To the hundreds of people in that writing community who crossed paths with me, I may not have named you, but I know you. There wouldn't be a me without a you.
- To every poor bastard who ever worked for me at any of my companies since the very first in 1991, if you're reading this, you may be entitled to compensation.
- To all the "stops" along the way, from grade-school teachers to college professors, from newspaper editors to rock guitarists, and the dozens of literary magazines that published my work so I could take this manuscript to publishers looking all official.

To my friends at The Tea Smith in Omaha for their generosity in supporting the launch of this book in my adopted hometown. To the communities that gave me another chance when I needed one most, thank you. You carried me further than I could have gone alone.

And to everyone I've missed by name: come to a reading and I'll hand-write your name right here in your copy of the book:

____

And Above All, To Elizabeth

To Elizabeth, who pushed me to create the time and space to finally try to become an author. For all the love, support, and patience you've given me, whether it was believing in this project long before I did or making our shared life the steady foundation from which I could leap into the unknown. You are the heart of everything I do, and any success I've found is because of you. Thank you for always pushing me to keep going, for knowing what I was capable of before I did, and for making me better, not just as an artist but as a person.

About the Author

Ryan T. Pozzi is primarily a nonfiction writer whose work also occasionally spans poetry, hybrid forms, and short fiction. He writes about legacy, failure, and the gap between the stories we tell and the messier truth underneath. *The Mess That Made Them* is his first book.

He didn't come to writing in a straight line. Growing up disabled and deeply self-conscious about it, he found his way into the world through books and music first, then through performance. As an adult he spent years building spaces where other people could make art, working, at various times, as a copywriter, journalist, poet, actor, director, producer, and the owner of a gallery and performance venue. He founded projects like the Nebraska Writers Collective and ran The Apollon, a multidisciplinary performance space in Omaha. On good nights, those rooms felt like proof that art could change the texture of ordinary life. On bad nights, the pressure of keeping everything afloat nearly broke him or maybe did break him depending on who you ask.

Eventually, the constant grind of nonprofit work, public expectation, and his own impossible standards caught up with him. After a long stretch of burnout and depression, he stepped away from public life and thought he might be finished with ambitious projects altogether. What stayed with him, though, was the question that had always bothered him beneath the success stories: why do we cling to the myth of singular genius when the real story is so much messier, and what does that myth do to the people who believe it.

At his wife's urging, he returned to the page, this time with less interest in performing certainty and more interest in telling the truth about how creative lives actually unfold. Writing became the next version of the work he had always done: trying to give people a place to see themselves more clearly and to feel less alone in their own chaos. *The Mess That Made Them* grew out of that turn. The book brings together his years of work in the arts, his early love of classical music, and his long, uneasy relationship with ambition into a single project that asks what it really costs to keep making things.

His shorter work has appeared in *Rattle*, *Fjords Review*, *Broad River Review*, *Northern New England Review*, and many others. He lives in Iowa, by way of Texas and Nebraska, with his wife, Elizabeth.

If this book met you somewhere in your own questions about work, art, or what to do with a life that hasn't gone the way you planned, he hopes you'll stay in touch. You can find him at ryantpozzi.com and on social media @ryantpozzi. For readers who want to keep thinking together about creative life, persistence, and the realities of trade publishing, he writes a free behind-the-scenes style newsletter, *Life on the Midlist*. Future books that tell more truth about our histories and the origins of both our best and worst ideas are already in various stages of drafting, research, and planning, and he would be glad to have you along for whatever comes next.

Also, isn't third-person writing neat? It sounded like someone was talking about me, but that was me the whole time. I'm right here. Love me or hate me, never forget I'm here if you need me. We're in this together.

Index